CAROLINE RENNOLDS MILBANK

Photographs by David Corio

HARRY N. ABRAMS, INC., PUBLISHERS, NEW YORK

For Rives

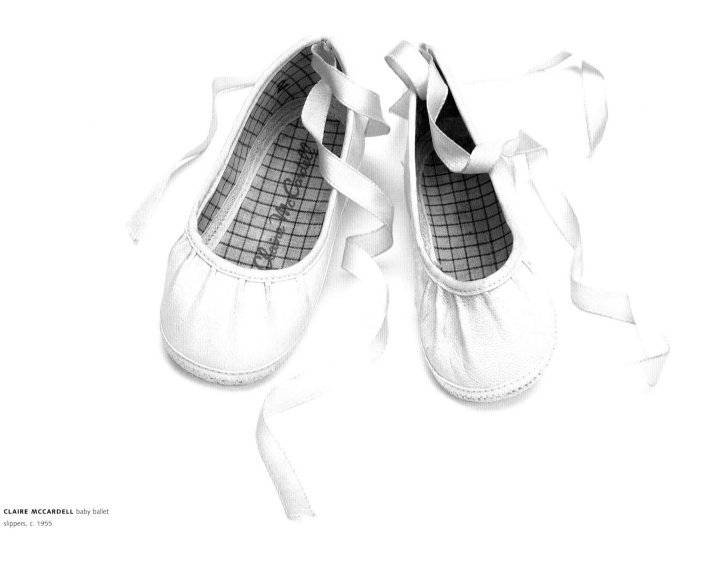

CLAIRE MCCARDELL baby ballet
slippers, c. 1955

CONTENTS

Paradigms of Fashion

While accessories, especially those created by fashion designers, can be and sometimes are functional, their real talent is to amuse. All of the reasons we wear clothes—to exude the pheromones that will accomplish propagation of the species, to display status, to express ourselves, to protect the body from the elements—are accomplished as well, if not better, by the perfect pair of stilettos, the latest must-have purse, the wittiest hat, or the most opaque sunglasses. Paradigms of fashion, these items can also provide insight into how designers work and how styles evolve. Crucial to the study of fashion is an examination of silhouette—as what changes most when fashion changes is the overall shape of what a woman (and to a lesser extent, a man) wears. A

In the nineteenth century, having one's clothes made was a full-time occupation, entailing repeated visits to separate establishments. In 1895, after being fitted for a reception dress at Worth, the preeminent couture house of the day, this flower-trimmed hat's former owner walked a few doors away, perhaps with dress fabric in hand, to commission matching headwear from posh milliners Maison Virot.

After Chanel's enormous success with costume jewelry beginning in 1924, couture accessories became big news, and big business. Rival couture houses quickly diversified. In 1928 *Women's Wear Daily* described this Lucien Lelong necklace and bracelet set as being set with "moonlight" cabochons.

change can be as large scale as bustles giving way to flat behinds and gigantic mutton sleeves, or as subtle as pants looking wrong with tapered hems. For the past century, most of the changes in Western fashion have been driven by couturiers and/or fashion designers who have introduced a new style at the exact moment when the world was ready for it, and it has taken hold. Many of these looks could not have taken flight without accessories to give them lift.

Such pieces provide an intriguing lens with which to examine fashion's evolution. The exoticism unleashed onto fashion a century ago by the Ballets Russes in Paris is evoked instantaneously by Paul Poiret's odalisque-printed fan. The Machine Age of the 1920s is exemplified by Jeanne Lanvin's streamlined lacquered aluminum purse. Elsa Schiaparelli's nervy surrealist fancies remind us that escapism was badly needed during the Depression Era. That there were at least two ways to look at feminine pulchritude during the late 1940s and early 1950s can be seen in the contrast between Roger Vivier's hair-thin heels, on which Christian Dior's New Look tottered, and Claire McCardell's snappily casual sunglasses.

What could 1960s Mods have worn with their minis if not Courrèges or Mary Quant boots? The liberated woman of the 1970s showed off an athletically trim figure in pared-down Halston, her waist not so much restrained as indicated by an Elsa Peretti belt. Chanel's opulent faux pearls and Byzantine gold filigree provide instant recall of 1980s glamour. The minimalism of the 1990s is personified by a Helmut Lang shopping bag of a purse. And with the turn of a new century comes the explosive growth of the idea of must-have objects, which pits classics like Chanel's quilted leather purse against the very latest thing, whose greatest appeal may be that it is ephemeral, doomed to last barely a season. One of the most endearing aspects of couturier accessories is that they are often made to wear just for one special effect—to render a single ensemble spectacular for a few runway moments.

The best fashion accessories act as microcosms of the designers' work. Madeleine Vionnet's mathematician side is revealed when she carves a rectangle away from the edge of a simple purse.

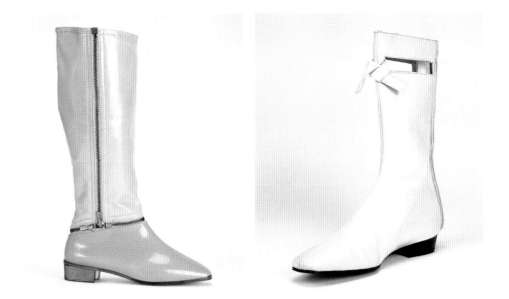

Mary Quant's rainboot of about 1967 was constructed of yellow knit fabric overlaid with clear vinyl.

Courrèges's white leather boot of the late 1960s featured a Velcro back closure.

Balenciaga's sense of sculpture is every bit as evident in one of his abstract shapes worn perched on the top of the head as in a ball gown. A simple knotted-cord bracelet subtly hand embroidered in beads sums up the dichotomy between monastic simplicity and post–Jet Age luxury in Giorgio Armani's work. John Galliano's amalgamation of found objects as might be worn by an imagined Parisian street person is part of a story he is telling through the (thanks to him, theatrical) medium of the runway.

Accessories give designers a chance to control a total look. How successful this can be is illustrated in the following anecdote from an American diplomat's memoir of his 1950s Paris stay. He describes having seen the Duchess of Windsor:

> She looked really smashing in the most amazing eye-opener of a beaded gown. Actually it was a shift made of thousands of dark red beads which must have weighed six hundred pounds. Dior had made the dress especially for this occasion. Reaching back to 1926, he had taken off the hook the most beaded of beaded nightgowns; this he had flung onto the Duchess's slip-of-a-girl body turning her into a stunning column of porphyry. The master touch was her necklace, which was a thick swirl of tightly wound green stones. Being a sort of dog collar, the necklace gave her a fine, barbaric look. Terribly chic! And the necklace caused more whispering, more amazement than either the Duchess or Dior could have hoped for. Obviously the stones had to be emeralds, uncut emeralds given her by some maharajah, or else purchased at untold cost from an Eastern potentate. Even those who thought the necklace hideous admitted that it was the key to the Duchess's attire.
>
> Subsequently it turned out to have cost fifty-eight dollars in Dior's own boutique. But he had made the Duchess promise to wear the red beaded dress only with the green glass dog collar.

On waiting lists since its introduction in 1996, and christened Lady Dior after being worn by Lady Diana, Princess of Wales, this monogram-charm-ornamented pocketbook went on to sell many more than 100,000 units.

With the success of John Galliano's latest version of a leather saddle bag, Dior has accomplished the desirable feat of offering both classic and brand-new must-haves simultaneously.

Although there are many forms of accessory made with rare and therefore precious substances, pieces concocted from humble materials have a particular charm. See, for example, Yves Saint Laurent's sautoir strung with peach pits, Geoffrey Beene's use of industrial tubing and rubber matting, and Issey Miyake's imposing sunglasses made of wood.

Designer accessories, like so many valid fashion ideas, owe their existence to Coco Chanel. In 1924 she showed an almost absurdly simple pair of faux-pearl earrings, one in white and one in black, and they became one of the success stories of the year. At a time when no woman went anywhere without her demure single strand of graduated pearls—whether real, induced, or man-made—Chanel brought a sense of chic to what had been considered more than a little déclassé: fake jewelry. Having begun as a milliner, she was already known for her hats, but after the success of one jewelry style after another, she branched out into silk flowers, gloves, and purses. Everything Chanel touched turned to gold, and many of these items not only have gained momentum as time passes, but have also become icons.

There were few designers who did not learn from Chanel's example. Just about every couture house in the 1920s and 1930s began to diversify. After diversification came licensing, and this type of arrangement spread like wildfire. Thus, today the relationship between the object signed with a designer's name and the designer's work is often obscure.

From earliest times and in every culture accessories have served as signifiers of status—not just in terms of their quality, and therefore cost, but also in terms of how they were worn. During the nineteenth century in Europe and the United States, an elaborate code of behavior dictating at what hour one wore the various accouterments with which one could adorn oneself, and how, reached its apogee. A lady participating in society's expectations learned how to mince in narrow slippers and manage at one time multiple objects, including a fan, a reticule or purse, a bouquet in a bouquet holder, a chatelaine, and a handkerchief. Strict rules governed which types of gloves to wear at which hour of the day, when a headdress was called for rather than a bonnet, what type

Chanel's famous quilted bag of the mid-1950s has been reinterpreted regularly over the years. This is a late-1990s version.

The beige satin material offsets the utilitarian design of Helmut Lang's shopping bag from the late 1990s.

For almost a year after Marc Jacobs showed apples and pears as part of his spring/summer 2001 line, pieces such as this apple-buckle belt were described by Internet vendors as "sold out."

of jewelry was appropriate for an unmarried woman to be seen in. So specific were the various codes that there developed "languages" of fan use, of flower symbolism, of wearing shawls (shadings of meaning could be seen in how a shawl was folded). Today, such associations with these items have all but vanished.

Back in the nineteenth century, and well into the twentieth, the hat was the accessory that could make grown women cry. Scarlet O'Hara acquiesced to Rhett Butler's proposal of marriage when she saw the bait: a Paris hat. Almost a hundred years after the Civil War, comic-strip wives went to mad lengths to hide millinery bills from their exasperated husbands. Today, other accessories have assumed covetous importance. While treated with derision, Imelda Marcos's footwear fetish coincided with growing acceptance of the idea of having a shoe habit.

Throughout much of the second half of the twentieth century, couture creations provided glamour and pertinence (in terms of disseminating new ideas) for fashion houses; sidelines like perfumes supplied the necessary cash flow. At the beginning of the twenty-first century, accessories are the engine that drives couture businesses. A must-have new item can singlehandedly revive a languishing older-name designer. Further, the idea that accessories are something not just to be worn, but also to be collected, has firmly taken hold. While it used to be that a particular item was desirable because it was new, playing hard to get has increasingly become a valuable marketing tool. Just a hint that a certain bag, or belt, or pair of boots is not available whets the purchasing appetite, particularly in a sluggish economy. On the Internet are purveyors who specialize in sold-out merchandise—the mere fact that a piece is unavailable adds to its allure. Today the thrill of the chase has almost supplanted the appeal of the object itself.

For fashion designers whose work revolves around their original textile design, the shape, or design of accessories often plays second fiddle to the signature fabrics from which they are made. Aside from his renowned pleating, Mariano Fortuny created mystical velvets and gauzes imbued with built-in patina from hand tinting and stenciling. From these, Fortuny fashioned such simply constructed accessories as drawstring bags, berets, doges' hats, flat scarves, and belts. Maria Monaci Gallenga, who specialized in stenciled velvets, created accessories in a range of styles, from frankly medieval headgear to fringed flapper shawls. Paco Rabanne, who had got his start working for couture jewelry maker Roger Jean-Pierre, took the technique of costume-jewelry construction a step further, making whole "fabrics" out of metal and plastic rings and links. These were startlingly novel when made into dresses. Emilio Pucci's prints, with their striking colors and boldly outlined patterns, are recognizable the world over. Zandra Rhodes's textile designs are not limited by the rectangle (the natural shape of work produced on a loom) but made in whatever form her imaginations takes.

Opposite, clockwise from top left:

Perugia flowerpot platform sandals, late 1930s, possibly made for Schiaparelli

Manolo Blahnik for John Galliano mules with wire-cage heels, autumn/winter 1995

Roger Vivier comma-heel evening shoes, autumn/winter 1963

Gripoix *pâte de verre* fish brooch, c. 1960, couturier unknown

Loulou de la Falaise for Yves Saint Laurent collar and cuff, c. 1992–93

Judith Leiber for Geoffrey Beene rhinestone *minaudière*, 1989

Below:

Elsa Peretti for Halston teardrop pendant, c. 1972

There has often been a symbiotic relationship between couturiers and the artisans who create jewelry, shoes, evening bags, and hats. Loulou de la Falaise has served as both muse and accessories designer for Yves Saint Laurent. Schiaparelli, in executing her various themed collections, relied on a multitude of talents, including Jean Schlumberger. Many who started out designing something special for a couture house went on to design under their own names, for example Perugia, who was discovered by Poiret; Fulco di Verdura, who first made jewelry for Chanel; Roger Vivier, originally associated exclusively with Christian Dior; and Elsa Peretti, who designed for Halston before moving to Tiffany & Co. Sometimes, but not always, the maker's identity is obvious: on closer inspection, Judith Leiber's distinctive pavé rhinestone minaudière turns out to be patterned with Geoffrey Beene's favorite dalmatian spots, and Gripoix's molten pools of glass are instantly recognizable, be they marked Chanel, Yves Saint Laurent, Givenchy, or any other name.

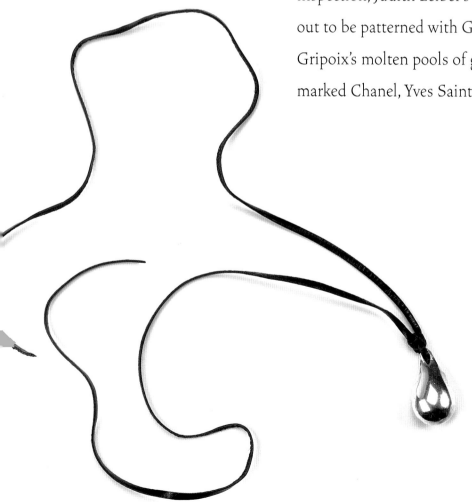

Twentieth-century art has invigorated fashion to no end. Yves Saint Laurent based entire collections on the cubism of Pablo Picasso and Georges Braque; in 1994, he made a bag in direct homage to Henri Matisse. Graffiti art inspired Stephen Sprouse's Day-Glo tights. Sprouse was known in the 1980s for reviving the miniskirt and for collaborating with Andy Warhol on a camouflage fabric pattern. Keith Haring designed the invitation for Vivienne Westwood and Malcolm McLaren's autumn 1983 Witches collection, as well as some of the fluorescent hieroglyphic prints used for the clothes. Brooches made in the shape of Haring's signature babies were pinned to many of the ensembles worn in the show. Modern abstract sculpture of the mid-twentieth century set out to render reductive geometric shapes monumental; like an office-plaza sculpture, Sybilla's shaped purse sets a cube on its edge. And Roy Lichtenstein's cartoon-edged brand of Pop Art surely influenced many items from the Chanel autumn/winter 2001 season.

"Surrealism is fashion's favorite art."

—RICHARD MARTIN

20

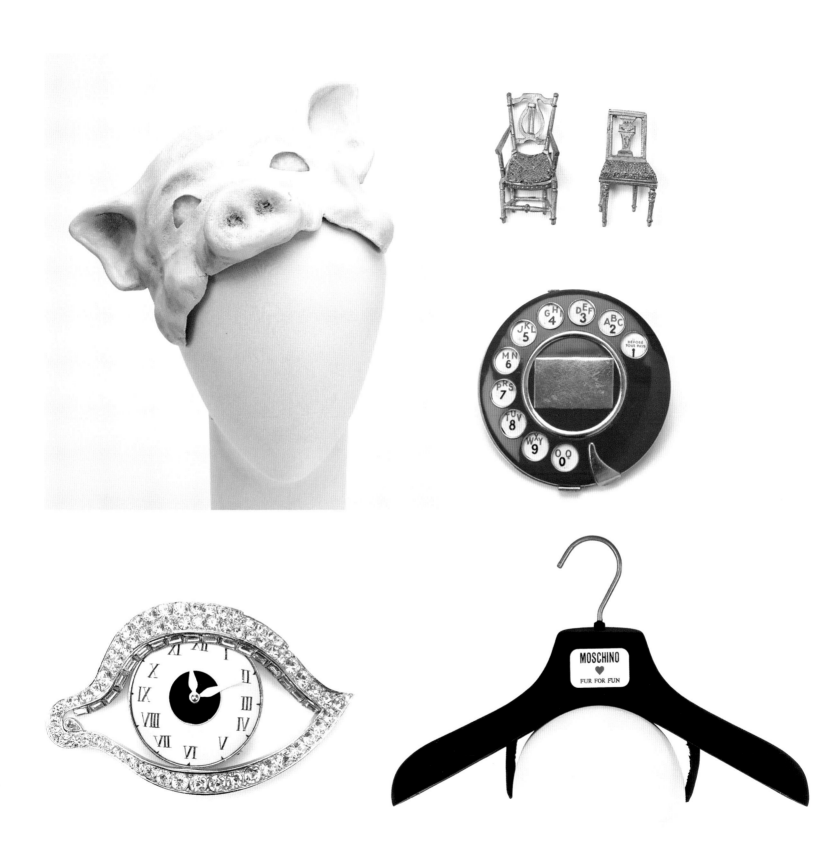

More winsome than logos are motifs that have been adopted by designers and will be forever associated with them: Dior's favorite flower, the fan Karl Lagerfeld is rarely without, Westwood's subversive appropriation of the symbol of the British crown, a cross for Lacroix in honor of his name, Yves Saint Laurent's peace doves (which have adorned several of the Christmas posters he designs every year), the toggle catch Bonnie Cashin adapted from the canvas roof of her convertible and went on to use everywhere, Patrick Kelly's buttons, Versace's Medusa, and, the queen of icons, Chanel herself.

Radical chic has its origins in the red bonnets and tricolor cockades worn in the French revolution. In more recent times, fashion has rejected politics per se in favor of pushing various envelopes. Recognizing that chic (and even novelty) is passé, Martin Margiella has explored ways of making us look at clothes in a new way, for example, translating a *tabi* sock into leather, and adding a heel, giving a familiar object a somewhat threatening air. (That his *tabi* boots have become icons in their own right, with lots of staying power, is ironic, given Margiella's sending up of must-have accessories: for fall 2002 he had a model walk the runway, holding up a purse enshrined in a glass box as if it were a museum exhibit.) Turning "unmentionables" into a choker and a necklace, Rifat Ozbek and Sonia Rykiel celebrated the end of an enduring taboo. Karl Lagerfeld's addition of teardrop pearls to screws made for wittily nervy earrings in the mid-1980s; that this sense of edginess is now fully mainstream became evident when Chanel and Dior favored such elements as razor blades and barbed wire over baroque pearls and diamanté.

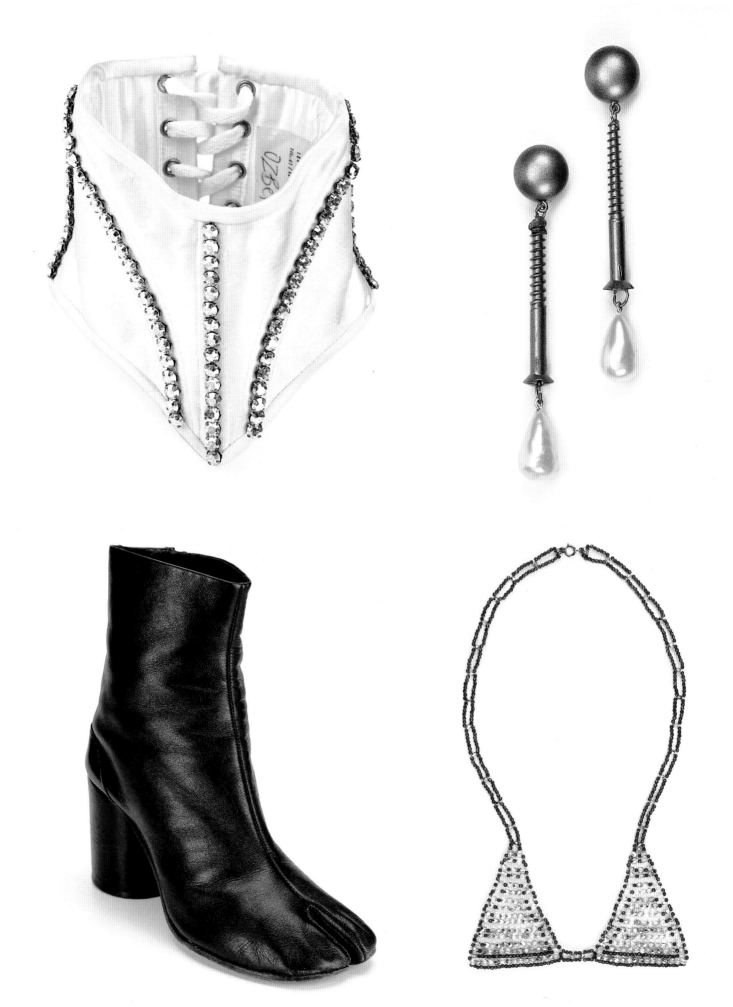

Opposite, clockwise from top left:

Geoffrey Beene shirt-sleeve taffeta scarf, autumn/winter 1994

Commes des Garçons flower-appliqué leather oxfords, 1990s

Diego della Valle for Geoffrey Beene man's dancing pump, autumn/winter 1988

Below:

Stephen Jones for John Galliano for Christian Dior satin corset hat, Haute Couture, autumn/winter 2000

As a general rule, most accessories are immediately identifiable as being made for a specific gender. When the lines blur, the borrowing tends to be one-sided: masculine items are most often translated for women rather than the other way around. A rare example of a merger is the hat below, in which a corset—that most feminine, not to mention intimate, of objects—has been crossed with a top hat—as the most formal masculine headgear, the corset's ideological opposite—creating an almost perfectly balanced demonstration of gender identity.

ADRIAN suede platform sandals,
early 1940s.
What could better accompany
Adrian's most typical creation, the
wide-shouldered narrow suit, than
shoes with platform soles?

Adrian

ONE OF THE MOST POIGNANT comments made by Gloria Swanson's character Norma Desmond in *Sunset Boulevard* (1950) was, "We had faces then." And it was true that, in the 1920s and 1930s, there was a convergence on the big screen between early cinematographers' skills, and the photogenic bone structure of the first movie stars, which resulted in images of glamour capable even of distracting the moviegoers from the privations of the Depression. As chief costume designer at the influential M-G-M studio, Adrian was pivotal in creating these images. Enormously talented as both an artist and costume designer, he may have been guided by his parents' background in millinery to emphasize the face. He was quick to see that especially in a close-up, a dramatic hat, necklace, or collar could draw the eye. One of his most renowned early designs was the Eugénie hat, tilted over one eye and adorned with plumes, which he made for Greta Garbo to wear in a 1930 movie called *Romance* that was set in the 1850s. It may have been the first time a movie style changed fashion everywhere: the streamlined 1920s cloche gave way to more romantic concoctions inspired by the Adrian model. • In 1942, Adrian opened his own fashion design business, producing custom-made and ready-to-wear collections sold from his own West Coast salon as well as nationally. The salon is remembered as the pinnacle of glamour by fashion designer Geoffrey Beene, who had escaped from medical school and was working at the time on the West Coast at the I. Magnin store in Beverly Hills. Decorated by Tony Duquette, Adrian's salon was, according to Beene: "very Grecian, very white, elegant, spare. The entrance was small, no clothes to be seen, just wonderful hats." Such hats, many produced by Mr. John, first known as a partner in the firm of John-Frederics, later by his own name, demonstrate Adrian's typical playfulness with proportion, an inclination toward wittiness, and a bold sense of color and silhouette.

Opposite, clockwise from far left:
ADRIAN beet-root-trimmed cartwheel hat, 1942.
This wide (just over 20 inches in diameter) cartwheel features beets fashioned out of feathers. Decorations such as these, which make up in amusement value what they may lack in workmanship or fine materials, reflect the reduced availability during World War II of imported materials and even, ultimately, of any but the most basic foods.

ADRIAN feathered headpiece, early 1940s.
Dramatically towering, this headpiece recalls the many scenes of showgirls on parade in Adrian-costumed films.

ADRIAN plumed toque, early 1940s.
Renowned for his costuming of historical films, Adrian possessed a knack for seeing the contemporary beauty in past designs. This toque looks thoroughly of its period yet evokes the drama of Roman helmets.

Left:
ADRIAN wide-brimmed hat with sugar-loaf crown, c. 1945.
A designer who would think of broadening Joan Crawford's shoulders (rather than try and minimize them) has a sense of the power of proportion.

AZZEDINE ALAÏA white-calf skirt belt, early 1990s.
There can be a fine line between skirts and belts in Alaïa's work.

Opposite:
AZZEDINE ALAÏA eyelet belt, spring/summer 1992.
Eyelet, a material that summons up images of the innocent side of lingerie, such as petticoats, camisoles, and little girl's pinafores, is translated here into rigid leather.

Azzedine Alaïa

AZZEDINE ALAÏA WAS ALREADY a trade secret when, in 1981, he debuted a small first collection that was an immediate *succès fou*. Striking decorative elements included zippers and the kind of lacing found on a boxing glove. On the long, fitted jackets of black leather suits, zippers went every which way; on black wool dresses, they spiraled around the body. Notable also were the pieces ornamented with grommets, including a wool beret, leather tunic coat, gauntlets, and handkerchief peplum belt. The gauntlets, whose cuffs were set with hundreds of small eyelets, seemed to personify a new kind of cutting-edge chic. Unbeknown to Alaïa, photojournalist Bill Cunningham, who had already shot images of the designer's clothes, spotted pieces from this seminal collection on the streets in Paris and photographed them for *Women's Wear Daily.* So impressed was Cunningham that he predicted that Alaïa's would be a "power that might have an influence for the last decades of this century, the kind of influence Balenciaga…inspired." • Known above all for designs that celebrate the body, Alaïa's oeuvre often makes reference, subliminally or overtly, to the act of dressing and undressing. Spiraling seams imply furling and unfurling. Gloves wrap around the arm like bandages. Lacing, seductively reminiscent of corsets, is a major leitmotif found in everything from evening dresses to hot pants, from long gloves to his much-copied ankle boots. Set in curves, Alaïa's lacing couldn't be less straitlaced. • Although Alaïa has shown his clothes with flats (*ballerines*), the typical Alaïa shoe has a heel height that will position a body in the most flirtatious posture. There is an undeniably saucy air to his platform pumps made with heels in the shape of a woman's derrière and legs, not to mention the ankle boots in black sticking out their red "tongues" from the top of the lacing. As always with Alaïa, sexiness is presented in a joyful way.

AZZEDINE ALAÏA FOR LOUIS VUITTON Centennial pocketbook, 1996.

Like a purse from 1940s or 1950s, this one, commisioned by Louis Vuitton to celebrate their monogram toile centennial in 1996, contains several items associated with ladylike grooming (cases for a comb, lipstick, and compact). Unlike its antique antecedents, it also contains a nod to present-day mores: a condom case.

AZZEDINE ALAÏA plexiglass
platform shoe, *jambe Naomi*,
spring/summer 1992.
The bottom and legs, erogenous
zones that sometimes seem to play
second fiddle to the bust, are celebrated here in one of the world's
great shoe designs, inspired by
Naomi Campbell.

AZZEDINE ALAÏA open-toed
platform espadrilles, spring/summer
1991.
Azzedine Alaïa told *Elle* magazine
that he had collaborated with artist
Julian Schnabel on the printed fabric
of these platform-espadrille hybrids.
Based on the signature shopping
bags of inexpensive Paris department store Tati, the oversize
houndstooth check was used for
whole ensembles as well as handbags, caps, long gloves, and various
styles of shoe.

GIORGIO ARMANI scarf necklace
of chain-link mesh with black
faceted beads and tassels, c. 1994.
Made in mesh, a necklace acquires
the throwaway chic of a scarf.

Giorgio Armani

GIORGIO ARMANI HAD BEEN IN BUSINESS for himself barely two years when his look—based on relaxed tailoring for men and women—took off. *Vogue* decreed his unstructured jacket "the Milan sensation." It was one of those Zeitgeist moments, establishing a new uniform for both sexes simultaneously. Clearly the way for modern women to dress was the way Armani saw them—in separates made of various menswear fabrics accompanied by slouchy hats, low-heeled shoes, and, an interesting choice for such contemporary clothes, almost quaint wrist-length gloves. • The Armani influence extended beyond tailoring to his monochromatic, organic palette and to his preferred materials: distinctive rayons and other new blends with texture, drape, and *flou*. This very particular feel for fabrics extended to his accessories as well. Naturally, soft hats like berets, newsboy caps, and skull caps were made of soft materials, but so were shoes, purses, and jewelry. First described as glass slippers in 1984, his plastic-sided shoes were often tipped with crepe de chine or velvet. Purses and pouches could be constructed of woven ribbon, braid, or string; sinuous jewelry derived from fishing line, knotted cords, rope, horsehair, and beads. Lapel flowers were updated in transparent silks or far-flung feathers. Near Eastern and Far Eastern influences made for pendants knotted onto long cords, belts made from rope, small purses in the shape of pouches or the Japanese *inro*. The Italian term *sprezzatura*—the art of making the difficult look easy—describes such beautifully crafted pieces that are the essence of ease.

Clockwise from top left:
GIORGIO ARMANI glass-bead choker with quartz pendant, 1998. In a muted desert palette, the contrast of textures stands out.

GIORGIO ARMANI coiled-cord earrings, 1994.
Cord, a pedestrian substance, is used to great effect to re-define chandelier earrings.

GIORGIO ARMANI black and white satin gloves, autumn/winter 1992.
Gloves—reminiscent of Victorian etiquette—often accompany Armani's modern designs. These were made to go with an evening dress whose strapless bodice consisted of two men's French cuffs precariously connected across the bust by the delicate chain of a cuff link.

Clockwise from right:

GIORGIO ARMANI plastic and velvet flat shoes, c. 1984. Throughout Armani's work is a sense that chic is closely aligned with comfort—as evident in his low-heeled and flat shoes, even for evening. The plastic-sided shoes, introduced in 1984, were to become classics, as befits descendants of Chanel's black-tipped sling-backs.

GIORGIO ARMANI gray silk and beaded-cord bracelet, c. 1990. Monochromatic and minimal in construction, this bracelet redefines elegance as a lack of pretension.

GIORGIO ARMANI suite of accessories—white raffia cap, embroidered-fabric sling-back mary janes, embroidered evening bag with wrist strap, white cord and *passementerie* tasseled belt, metal and bead drop earrings—spring/summer 1993. Symphony in off-white: this group of pieces was worn with an ivory strapless long dress from a collection that featured Moroccan, North African, and Turkish influences.

BALENCIAGA navy stripped-feather spiral pillbox hat, early 1950s.
The hard edges of the pillbox, a design for which Balenciaga was famous, are blurred in a haze of stripped feathers

Balenciaga

THE MORE DRAMATIC a couture dress, the less likely it is
that conventional jewelry—precious stones, in conservative settings—will look
appropriate. Balenciaga's works of mobile architecture rarely lacked for drama. Although he never developed
a boutique line brimming with every kind of accessory, he did, from his first Paris collection on, show clothes with pieces
designed to complement them. "Balenciaga does pearls well, five or six strands, all the same length, twisted together," as *Harper's*
Bazaar reported. Next to receive attention were pieces made of jet, recalling the same Spanish heritage he mined for embroideries.
Later costume jewelry choices, made by Robert Goossens and Roger Jean-Pierre, tended toward the bold and the baroque—heavy
gilt settings, smoky rhinestones, rough-cut turquoises. Hearts were a favorite motif; in 1961, *Vogue* salivated over a "jet heart-
throb of a clip." • Throughout the 1930s and into the 1940s, Balenciaga's accessories reflected a strong strain of
Victorianism, which showed itself in his clothes in his use of jet embroideries, rich guipure laces, scrolling appliqués,
and full, sweeping skirts, aprons, and capelets. Straight out of *Godey's Lady's Book* might have come his tortoise-
shell hair comb, jet dog collars, drawstring purses made of ribbons, pouch purses designed to be hung from
a belt, miniature miser's purses, and flower-trimmed hats, made of black horsehair and designed to
be worn low on the brow. This feeling was still going strong in 1947 when *Vogue* featured an
evening bag made by Lenthéric for Balenciaga: a "once in a lifetime bag of black
satin, richly embroidered in gold, caught with a gold cord. (It comes
in Balenciaga's own little hatbox.) $250.00."

ROBERT GOOSSENS FOR
BALENCIAGA gilt-metal and rhinestone necklace, 1960s.
While this necklace looks substantial, it is as flexible as a silk ribbon.

As Balenciaga's designs became more purely sculptural, the Victorian influence fell by the wayside. In *Paris à la Mode,* Celia Bertin describes an intimate fashion show at the house of Balenciaga (until the 1980s it was the practice for couture houses to hold continual small showings of their most recent models): "I count half-a-dozen of them as they pass by, proud, aloof, with lifted profiles, looking above the heads of the customers. They wear curious hats, designed by M. Balenciaga to go with his dresses, each made from a single flower or some veiling, or perhaps from a big felt shape. These hats, which they wear stuck straight on to their foreheads or the backs of their heads, are not intended to make them prettier, but to complete a bold and perfect architecture."

Even sprouting a lead-pony egret, Balenciaga hats were never frivolous. Shapes were the essence of shape—whether pillbox, cap, crown with no brim, coif, or veil. Materials tended to the extremes of soft, such as feathers, organza, and tulle, or hard, as in patent leather, crisp straw, gazar, and suede. Fabrics were often unexpected—in 1948 he made a small flat boater of apricot leather to go with an apricot coat. In 1955, *The New York Times* pictured a hat described as one of "this designer's sly shockers: white fox head with diamond eyes and pink satin bow in his mouth." When, in the early 1950s, Balenciaga began easing the lines of a suit or a dress away from the body, his hats began to stand away from the head as well. Sculptural, neat-domed, crownless hats were shown along with lampshades, poufs, cloches, and buckets. Balenciaga was rarely associated with shoes, as most of his clothes required rather plain footwear, yet *The New York Times* did report in 1967 that "the man who first made boots chic is now bored with them."

Balenciaga closed his couture department in 1968, four years before his death. The business continued, offering perfumes and some accessories, such as sunglasses and logo-decorated goods, along with fashions designed by Michel Goma and then Josephus Thimister. In 1995, Nicholas Ghesquière joined the company and quietly began to make waves. His designs, including his 2001 *succès fou,* the lariat bag, have been much coveted and much copied, earning him a place among leaders of fashion.

ROBERT GOOSSENS FOR BALENCIAGA brooch with red beads, rhinestones, and *pâte de verre* center stone, 1960s. When choosing jewels from artisans such as Robert Goossens, Balenciaga veered toward bold shapes and colors.

RENÉ SCHNERB FOR BALENCIAGA medallion evening bag, 1939. This compact/purse was designed to dangle from the wrist, by what *Vogue* called a "beguiling bow-knot of black ribbon."

BALENCIAGA lead-pony hat,
1953.
In this hat, the pale blush-pink silk
satin fabric is smoothed out over a
foundation of tulle over straw, then
released in a twisted tuft that acts
as an exclamation point.

Left:
BALENCIAGA ruby satin evening purse, 1950s.
Like many a Balenciaga ball gown, this evening purse combines a strong shape with a dramatic color.

Opposite, clockwise from top left:
Cocktail hat, autumn/winter 1951, attributed to **BALENCIAGA**.
Typically Balenciaga is the contrast between the severe black velvet disk and the softly furled pink silk rose nestled in a froth of ostrich feathers.

BALENCIAGA white-tulle *mille-feuille*s hat, spring/summer 1964.
Here an almost architectural structure is created using the softest of materials, tulle, made in circles that form densely layered shapes.

BALENCIAGA feathered hat, autumn/winter 1950.
Originally made for Babe Paley, this plush hat with black ostrich feathers recalls those worn in Old Master paintings.

BALENCIAGA curly-ostrich-feather hat, autumn/winter 1962.
Reminiscent of Balenciaga dresses sewn overall with ostrich fronds, this hat features a particularly subtle detail: the underhat is pale, pale blue, giving the feathers as they move the faintest hint of sky.

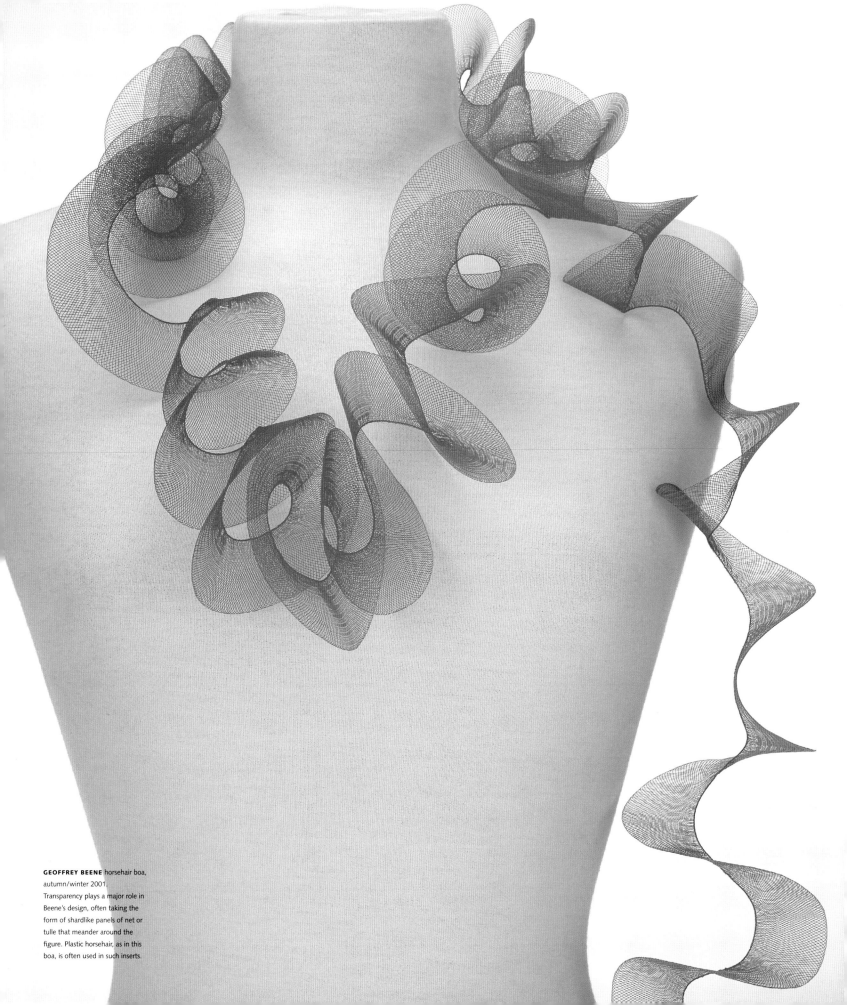

GEOFFREY BEENE horsehair boa, autumn/winter 2001. Transparency plays a major role in Beene's design, often taking the form of shardlike panels of net or tulle that meander around the figure. Plastic horsehair, as in this boa, is often used in such inserts.

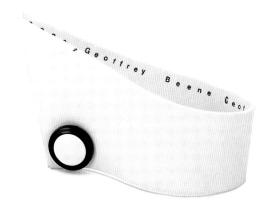

Geoffrey Beene

AT THE BEGINNING of his career, in the 1960s, Geoffrey Beene's simple, striking clothes were occasionally shown in fashion magazines with hats by master American milliners Lilly Daché or Mr. John, usually made of a matching fabric and in a strong sculptural shape—helmet or rounded pillbox with top knot. Also made to match were ankle-bone boots in the same sequined argyle as a sleeveless mini dress, these by Beth Levine for Herbert Levine. As his business grew, so did various licensing arrangements, for scarves, shoes, a costume-jewelry line for Kramer, which surfaced during the 1970s. In the 1980s, Fratelli Rosetti, Andrew Geller, and Diego della Valle made shoes for the Beene Bag line, and Judith Leiber produced evening bags for Geoffrey Beene. Jewelry and accessory artisans such as Stephen Dweck, Cara Croninger, and James Arpad have designed pieces for him. • It is often said of a well-cut dress that it fits like a glove. There is something exquisite about the way Beene contrasts slightly wrinkled, not-quite-fitting gloves with his second-skin dresses and jumpsuits. Rarely are Beene designs, from the barest to the most demure, shown without hand coverings—and they run the gamut, from wrist length to gauntlet to thirty-button made in point d'esprit, gingham checks, men's shirting stripes, stretch satin, or jersey. While many of these fabrics are venerable classics of American fashion and the haute couture, Beene also has an eye for the beauty inherent in functional industrial supplies. Clear plastic tubing filled with different colors of sand make belts for his liquid jersey dresses; neoprene sheets can be fashioned into petals for necklaces, or cuffs into bracelets. Flowers from a silk print, laminated and sprinkled with rhinestones, result in the most contemporary of corsages. As Geoffrey Beene has pared down his fashions, ever working toward the goal of making clothes that are distilled to the very essence of design, his former signature elements—Peter Pan collars, vest-point midriffs, sparkling white cuffs—have floated free and become discrete accessories, morphing into necklaces, belts, and bracelets.

GEOFFREY BEENE neoprene cuff, spring/summer 1998. Pristine white cuff, representing the bourgeois ideal of propriety, are here updated in space-age materials.

Opposite, clockwise from top left:
GEOFFREY BEENE plastic bracelet with disk flower, autumn/winter 1997.
GEOFFREY BEENE Lucite disk necklace, autumn/winter 1999.
GEOFFREY BEENE rubber and neon plastic necklace, autumn/winter 1999.
GEOFFREY BEENE neoprene pierced-disk collar, autumn/winter 1997.
Like modern architects of the late twentieth century, Beene has appreciated the appeal of industrial materials, sometimes transforming Canal Street discoveries into runway high points.

Above:
GEOFFREY BEENE velvet Scrunchie bracelets, autumn/winter 1998.

The designing eye sees possibility everywhere. Here the ubiquitous hair Scrunchie, purchased on the street, has been transformed into lush bracelets that ooze glamour.

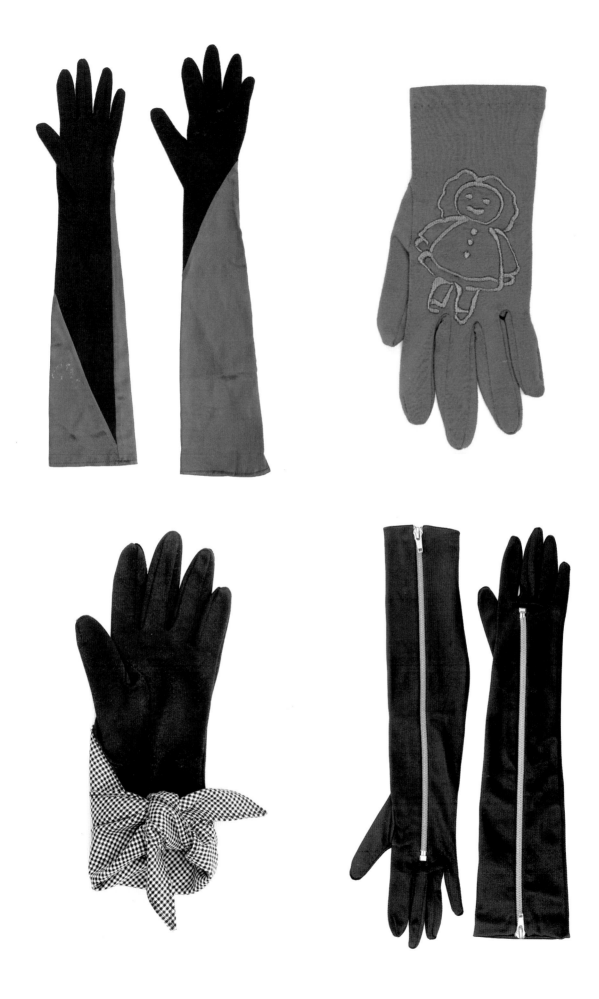

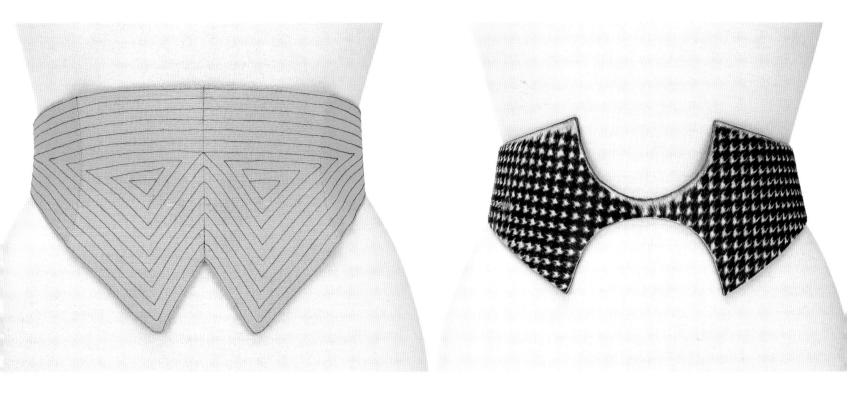

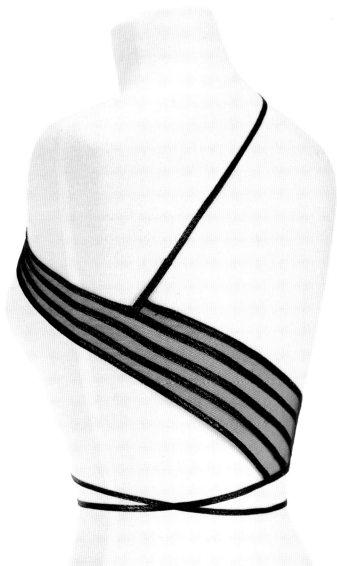

Opposite, clockwise from top left:
GEOFFREY BEENE satin and wool long gloves, autumn/winter 1990.

GEOFFREY BEENE embroidered jersey gloves, spring/summer 1994. Beene's impish side rears itself in gloves embroidered with little girls.

GEOFFREY BEENE satin zipper gloves, spring/summer 1999. Industrial zippers in bright colors evoke Schiaparelli.

GEOFFREY BEENE cotton handkerchief-tied glove, spring/summer 1987.
Beene's allegiance to his American roots shows in his frequent use of gingham.

Gloves are the quintessential Beene accessory, emitting sparks not only of the languidly glamourous 1930s but also of Victorian days when a lady never went anywhere without the proper hand covering.

This page, clockwise from top left:
GEOFFREY BEENE *gazar* belt, spring/summer 1988.
Beene's signature rows of topstitching on *gazar* give definition to a belt that ends in vest/collar points.

GEOFFREY BEENE shaped belt, autumn/winter 1995.
Waists play an important role in Beene's body-conscious designs. This midriff-framing belt plays a conventional houndstooth pattern against the texture of haired calfskin.

GEOFFREY BEENE harness/belt of black tulle and braid, autumn/winter 1998.
Harold Koda has described such Beene harnesses as this as devices that "overlay, segment, and define the torso."

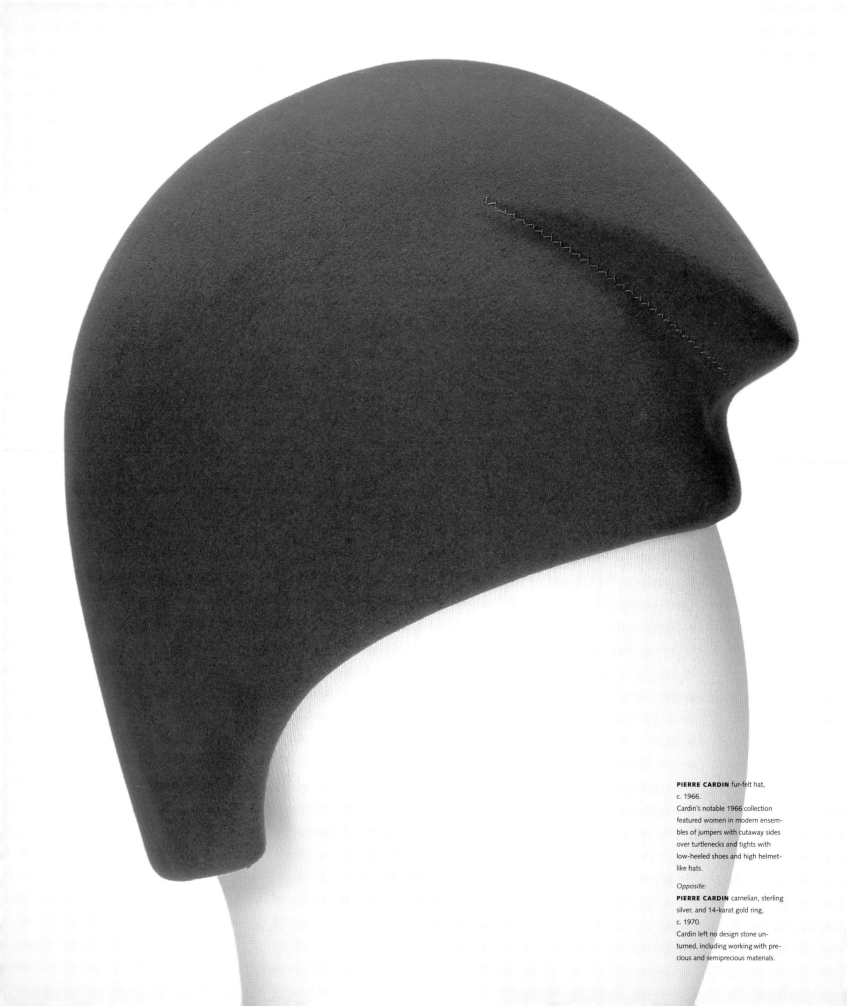

PIERRE CARDIN fur-felt hat,
c. 1966.
Cardin's notable 1966 collection
featured women in modern ensembles of jumpers with cutaway sides
over turtlenecks and tights with
low-heeled shoes and high helmetlike hats.

Opposite:
PIERRE CARDIN carnelian, sterling
silver, and 14-karat gold ring,
c. 1970.
Cardin left no design stone un-
turned, including working with precious and semiprecious materials.

Pierre Cardin

CARDIN'S EARLIEST WORK was gently sculptural; he was among the pioneers who devised clothes in relaxed shapes, often in heavy fabrics, that eased the 1950s silhouette away from the body. In the 1960s, he embraced the Space Age wholeheartedly, dressing men and women in jumpsuits, boots, and helmets, or knit tights and tops with vinyl breastplates or belt skirts. Geometry played a prominent role in his futuristic vision: scallops, zigzags, and bull's-eyes proliferated. Early accessories included boldly simple sculptural hats, along with such elegantly inventive pieces as a brooch made of large faux diamonds mounted on carpenter's nails. Pears, probably in a play on the designer's first name, often appeared as brooches or pendants. • When he made the cover of *Time* magazine, in 1974, clad only in a towel and boots, holding an electric razor, standing next to a chair and mirror, all by Pierre Cardin, it was big news—and the first time that a designer had branched out quite so far. As *Time* put it, the designer's PC monogram was "flaking all over the globe like chic graffiti." Cardin was hardly the first couturier to place his monogram on his designs—that honor goes to Jean Patou, or, perhaps more compellingly, Coco Chanel. But Cardin was the first to demonstrate the breadth and power of an instantly recognizable symbol like a logo. At the end of his career, his most lasting influence will have been his demonstration of the potency of the designer-as-brand.

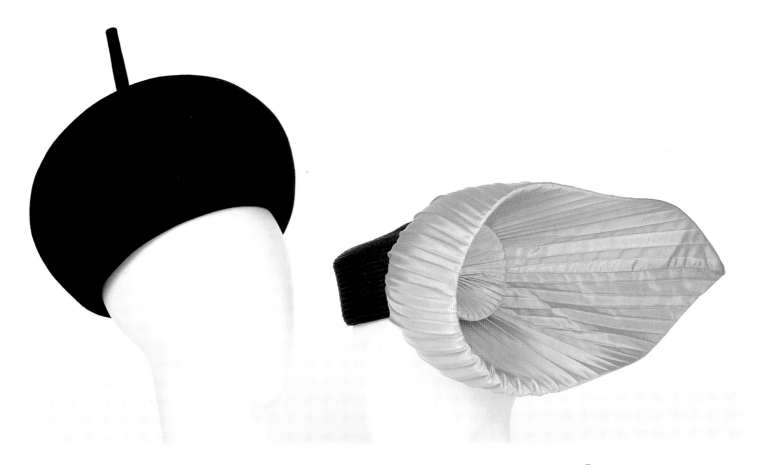

Opposite:
PIERRE CARDIN beaded evening
bags, 1970.
Op Art contributed to a love of geometric patterns in the 1960s and
1970s. While very much of their moment, these bags recall similar examples from the 1910s and 1920s.

Clockwise from top left:
PIERRE CARDIN balloon hat with
beret ferrule, autumn/winter 1990.
Cardin first showed a ballooning
beret in 1964; the example here
(left) is from his Haute Couture collection, autumn/winter 1990.

PIERRE CARDIN black straw pillbox
with pleated silk "quill," 1980s.
In the late 1970s and early 1980s,
Cardin added pleated elements to
his sculptural designs. As can be seen
in this hat (right), the airiness of the
pleating contrasted with the bold-
ness of the shapes created from it.

PIERRE CARDIN metal and Lucite
sautoir, late 1960s.
As befits a Space Age design, this
simple sautoir incorporates the
brand-new (in the 1960s) test-tube
material Lucite.

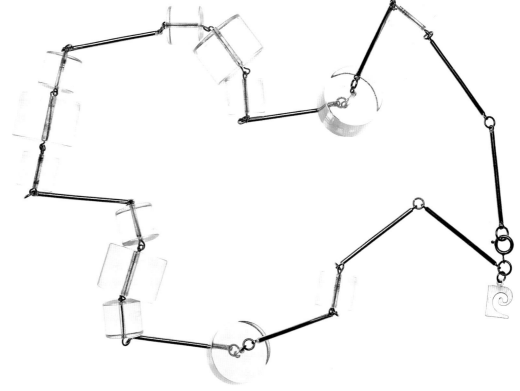

CHANEL quilted-leather bag, mid to late 1950s.
From Chanel's 1920s forays into purse design came such elements as quilting, chain handles, and the use of unusual fabrics like jerseys and tweeds. All would resurface when she produced what would become the definitive Chanel purse in 1955. Instantly a classic, its appeal has hardly dimmed in half a century.

CHANEL (GABRIELLE CHANEL, FRENCH, 1883–1971)
HOUSE ESTABLISHED 1913

Chanel

IRONICALLY FOR A COUTURIÈRE whose impact would be simply enormous, Gabrielle (Coco) Chanel's career built steam in an almost haphazard manner. She had begun, in 1910, as a milliner, yet her cardigan sweaters, first shown around 1913, were what everyone *had* to have. Young women thought her subsequent straight-line jersey chemises made dressing so easy (and their elders didn't know what to make of them). Then, in 1924, Chanel single-handedly created a whole new category of couture must-haves when she borrowed a page from Max Beerbohm's novel *Zuleika Dobson* and set off a craze for pearl earrings, one white and one black. Next to capture attention was her choker of large baroque pearls worn high on the neck, which *Vogue* featured in five separate fashion photographs and/or drawings in 1924. Although it is difficult to know from the surviving black-and-white sketches exactly what the first generation of Chanel pearl designs looked like, written descriptions (of black and white pearls strung with green, blue, or red glass beads in lengths ranging from choker to sautoir) indicate they were probably made by Gripoix in what would be deemed one of the most successful artisan/couture collaborations ever. Given the mores of the times—anything but a single strand of graduated "real" pearls in the daytime was considered vulgar—the success of these frankly faux jewels, worn with dresses made out of the same material as men's underwear, was astonishing. • Soon joining the pearls in popularity were "Chanel crystals," clear stones mounted in silvertone metal, made in all lengths and worn with her deceptively simple little silk frocks. By 1927, the crystals were so ubiquitous that *Women's Wear Daily* described a Lanvin purse as having an ornament of Chanel jewels. The trade paper also reported that Chanel jewelry regularly out-sold all other faux jewels. Two designers would become associated with Chanel's modern-style jewelry; Count Etienne de Beaumont, who had begun working with her in 1924, and Paul Iribe, whose 1932 designs of real diamond shooting stars, bowknots, and other pieces were exhibited in her house. • By the end of the 1920s, pieces described as gypsylike, hinting of Byzantine, Mughal, or

KARL LAGERFELD FOR CHANEL
crystal cross, Haute Couture, autumn/winter 1992, probably made by **GRIPOIX**.
While the style of this cross reflects Chanel's personal taste, its scale reflects the rapper fashions of the 1990s.

Renaissance taste, began to appear, perhaps inspired by a new collaborator, Fulco di Verdura. In 1934, *Women's Wear Daily* described designs by Verdura for Chanel as "gold earrings studded with multi-colored gems … matched by large brooches and hat ornaments, all done in 18K gold, with genuine gems, [which] very much suggest antique Hungarian or Check [sic] jewelry." Verdura, who would become a great (real) jeweler in his own right, was responsible for Chanel's famous enameled cuffs, set with Maltese crosses, starbursts, or arrangements of stones.

The public became increasingly fascinated with, and influenced by, how Chanel herself dressed. In 1923, *Vogue* published a photograph of Chanel "whose designs are as youthful and chic as herself," wearing a grosgrain hat pinned with a double-sided pearl brooch and pearl earrings. In 1931, Chanel made her first visit to the United States, to work on costumes for Samuel Goldwyn. Her travel costume was noted down to the last carefully coordinated detail: with her ermine-collared beige tweed sporty suit she wore beige suede gloves, beige and white single-strap shoes, and a pearl necklace, hat ornament, and earrings. At a reception in New York in April, her simple white satin long dress was accented with "gypsy bracelets in multicolored stones in quantity on both arms, and a long necklace of the same stones in combination with her pearls." By 1937, Chanel evening dresses were regularly being shown on models accessorized in exactly the same way as Mademoiselle: with veiled headdresses, gold and pearl and stone necklaces piled on top of each other, ornate belts, and Verdura's striking cuffs.

After her singular style, perhaps Chanel's greatest genius was her invention or adoption of a group of idiosyncratic accessories that seem incapable of ever going completely out of fashion. Her long strings of crystals and/or pearls appeared year

after year. The first version of her quilted pocketbook appeared in 1927, the prototype for the contemporary version in 1955. She showed a tweed bag in 1928, a knit purse in 1929. The black bow in the hair and the two-tone shoe came into use during the 1930s. Silk flowers, which she had used in the 1920s to punctuate her streamlined designs, were a motif she never abandoned, though gradually, during the 1930s, she came to favor the camellia. When, after her World War II–induced retirement, she reopened her couture house in 1954, she added to her stable of signature pieces new elements, such as chain-link straps for the quilted bags and lion's faces and double-C logos for buttons. She continued to work with Gripoix on poured-glass and other jewelry styles, and she collaborated with Robert Goossens on Byzantine- and Renaissance-inspired jewels wrought in gilt metal. Her black-tipped sling-back shoes were produced by Raymond Massaro and René Mancini.

After Chanel died in 1971, Diana Vreeland described her as having embodied "the spirit of the twentieth-century woman. She was a most important woman. I'm not talking about the pill and abortion and all the things that have helped women *now* that they're free. She freed them. She gave them the momentum and the style." The house of Chanel experienced a fallow period during the 1970s and was just beginning to invigorate itself in the area of accessories under Frances Patiky Stein's stewardship when, in 1983, Karl Lagerfeld was signed on to design first the couture and then the ready-to-wear lines. Lagerfeld's brilliant riffs on elements from the Chanel archive have been as influential, meaningful, and coveted as the originals were in their time. As Bernadine Morris wrote in *The New York Times*: "When it comes to turning classics on their heads and making them look like the cutting edge of fashion, Lagerfeld has no match."

CHANEL FOR ARIS ivory kid street gloves, autumn/winter 1929. The earliest forms of licensing, of which these gloves are a rare example, involved couture houses teaming up with manufacturers. The first ad touting the new Aris gloves by Chanel (appearing in August 1929) deliberately obscured the gloves, building excitement (and preventing copying) by stating that the actual design would not be revealed until later. The advertisement's subliminal message was that a couture name like Chanel was a valuable promotional tool.

CHANEL black silk and tulle evening headdress, c. 1937. "Says Mademoiselle Chanel: 'A woman is a little thing beside a man. When I go to the theatre I see in the row ahead of me the tall, arrogant men with their shiny hair, and then beside them the little insignificant figures of the women. Therefore, since I don't care for evening hats, I have made these head-dresses to give her height, to make her more of a person, more important.' "

CHANEL jewel-set calfskin belt, autumn/winter 1932. As early as 1926, Chanel had great success with tailored, yet jeweled, belts. This 1932 example typifies her tendency, way ahead of its time, to blur the lines between night and day.

GRIPOIX FOR CHANEL *pâte de verre* necklace, c. 1938. Classic Gripoix and classic Chanel: metal outlines filled in with *pâte de verre*. This version of an ancient technique was developed by Maison Gripoix in homage to Mughal jewelers' techniques, particularly the use of luminously transparent backless-set gems.

CHANEL crystal sautoir, c. 1930. Chanel's 1920s jewel designs had been spectacularly simple. This sautoir, attributed to Gripoix, hints of the greater complexity to come in the 1930s.

Left to right:

CHANEL gilt-metal star necklace, 1939.
By the late 1930s, Chanel's neck-laces had grown from single-strand chokers and sautoirs into bibs. A piece like this was deemed by *Vogue* in 1939 to be a "spectacular ornament … for a day dress."

CHANEL gilt-metal necklace, c. 1937.
Images of this necklace appeared in *Vogue*, *Harper's Bazaar*, *L' Officiel*, and in an ad for Hattie Carnegie, possibly New York's most exclusive specialty store. *Harper's Bazaar* de-scribed it as "a golden plastron of birds and flowers"

Opposite, clockwise from top:
CHANEL faux-pearl and rhinestone sautoir, 1960s, attributed to **GRIPOIX**.
CHANEL faux-emerald-set earrings with pearl drops, c. 1960, probably executed by **ROBERT GOOSSENS**.
CHANEL faux-pearl-and-ruby-bead sautoir, 1960s.
CHANEL pendant/brooch (pin removed), late 1950s.
ROBERT GOOSSENS FOR CHANEL hinged snake bangle bracelet, c. 1962–69.
ROBERT GOOSSENS FOR CHANEL cross pendant with bezel-set stones, late 1960s.
ROBERT GOOSSENS FOR CHANEL faux-pearl bar brooch/pendant, c. 1961.
ROBERT GOOSSENS FOR CHANEL faux-pearl ear clips, c. 1960.
ROBERT GOOSSENS FOR CHANEL gilt-metal and green-glass-bead bangle bracelet, c. 1962–69.

Hardly an image of a Chanel suit, or cocktail dress, or coat appeared in a fashion magazine during Chanel's comeback years without being adorned by one or many, usually many, of the types of items pictured here. The pearl-centered earrings, bar brooches, sautoirs, and bracelets were classics—the cross-centered gilt-filigree pendant set with green poured glass was one of Chanel's favorite pieces and the faux-pearl earrings are similar to ones in which then-First Lady Jacqueline Kennedy was often photographed.

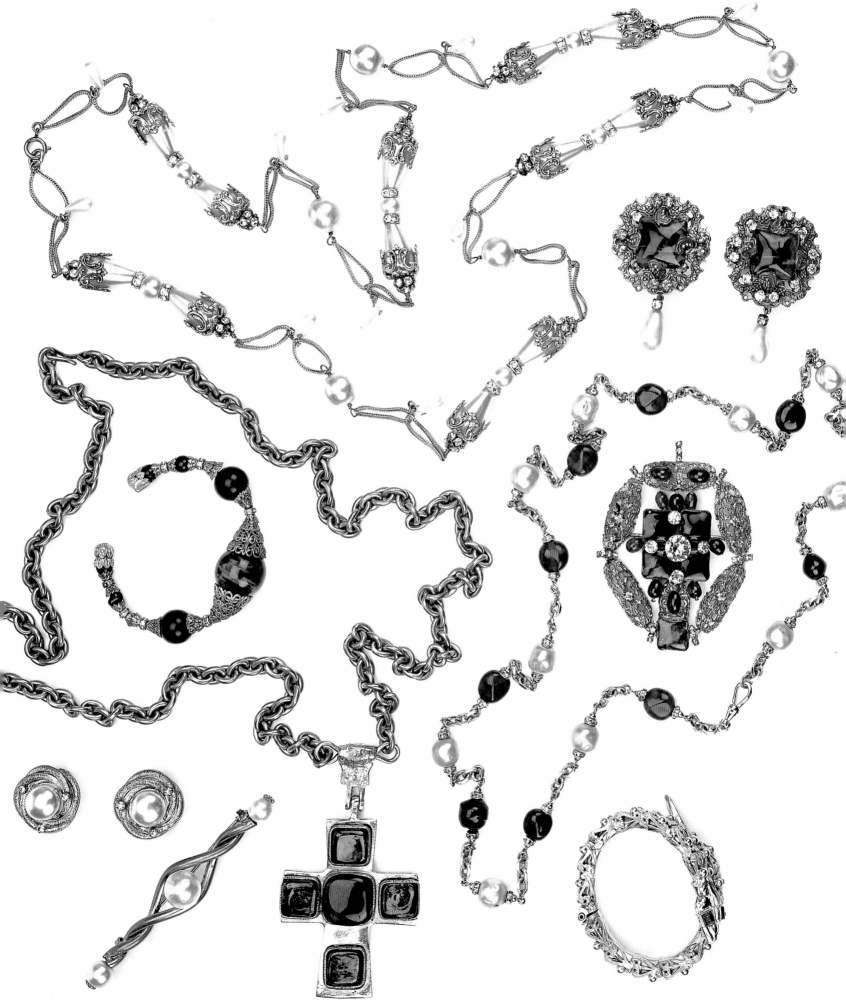

Clockwise from above:

MASSARO FOR CHANEL sling-back shoes, c. 1960.
Chanel was often photographed during the 1920s and 1930s in what were known as spectator pumps, two-tone and decorated with perforations. She revived elements of this sporty look in the 1950s when she developed two distinctive styles of two-tone shoes. Aside from the contrasting toe as shown here, there was another look with contrasting triangular insert at the toe.

GRIPOIX FOR CHANEL faux-pearl sautoir with *pâte de verre* pendant, 1983.
Coming on the heels of the minimalist 1970s, Chanel jewelry of the 1980s looked richly opulent, beautifully made, and, above all, "new." Many pieces were based directly on archival designs by Chanel and Gripoix.

KARL LAGERFELD FOR CHANEL gold-painted cuff with faux pearls and glass stones, spring/summer 1990.
The 1990s saw the Chanel scale grow bolder and bolder.

KARL LAGERFELD FOR CHANEL
gingham mules, c. 1999.
So potent is the Chanel mystique
that even the ribbon off a perfume
package holds allure. Such a ribbon
ornaments a pair of mules, the favorite shoe of the late 1990s.

KARL LAGERFELD FOR CHANEL
patent leather, Lucite, and faux-
pearl mules, spring/summer 1992.
Of all the elements associated forever with Chanel, perhaps the most
indelible are pearls, her first great
success.

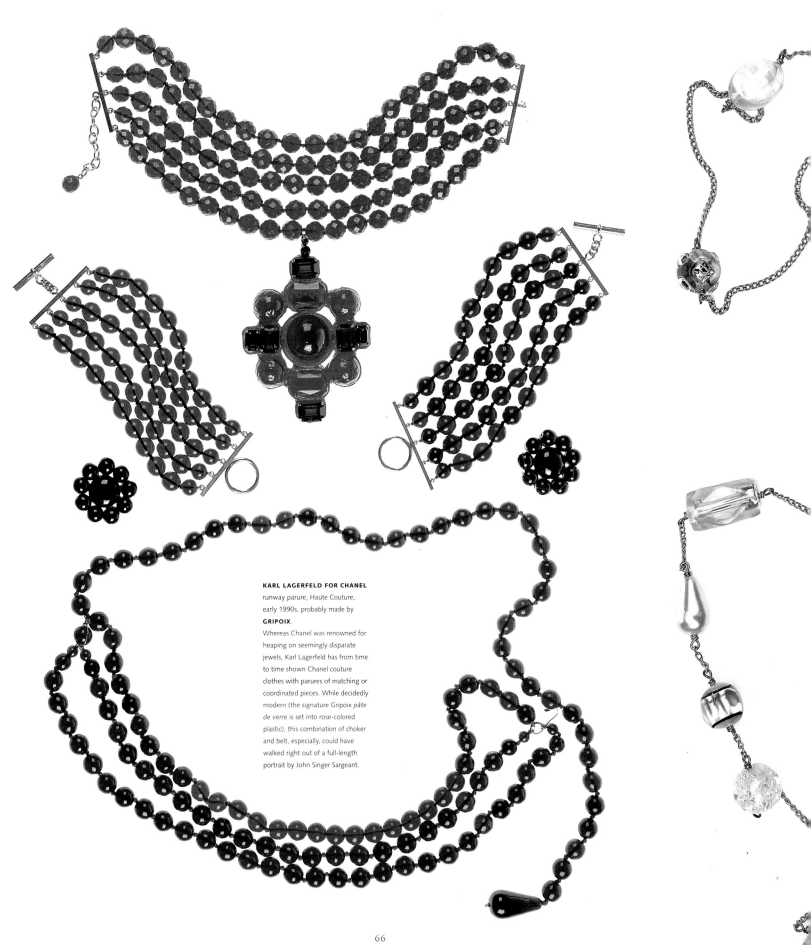

KARL LAGERFELD FOR CHANEL
runway parure, Haute Couture,
early 1990s, probably made by
GRIPOIX.
Whereas Chanel was renowned for
heaping on seemingly disparate
jewels, Karl Lagerfeld has from time
to time shown Chanel couture
clothes with parures of matching or
coordinated pieces. While decidedly
modern (the signature Gripoix *pâte
de verre* is set into rose-colored
plastic), this combination of choker
and belt, especially, could have
walked right out of a full-length
portrait by John Singer Sargeant.

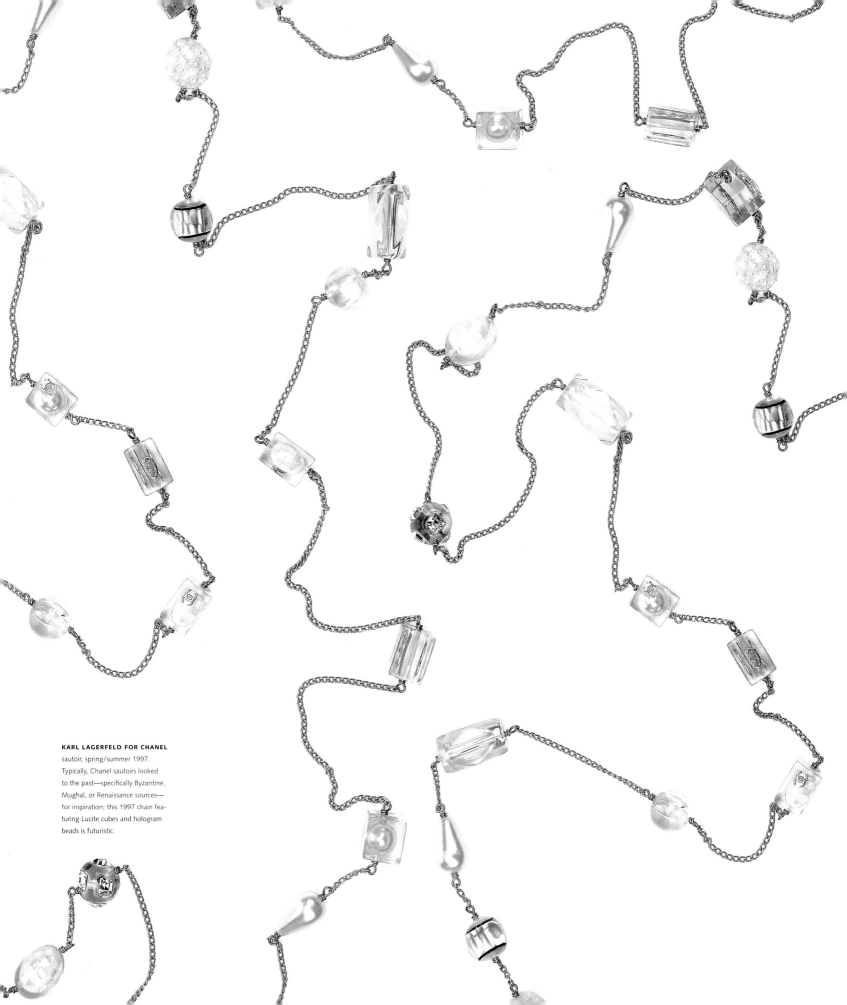

KARL LAGERFELD FOR CHANEL
sautoir, spring/summer 1997.
Typically, Chanel sautoirs looked
to the past—specifically Byzantine,
Mughal, or Renaissance sources—
for inspiration; this 1997 chain featuring Lucite cubes and hologram
beads is futuristic.

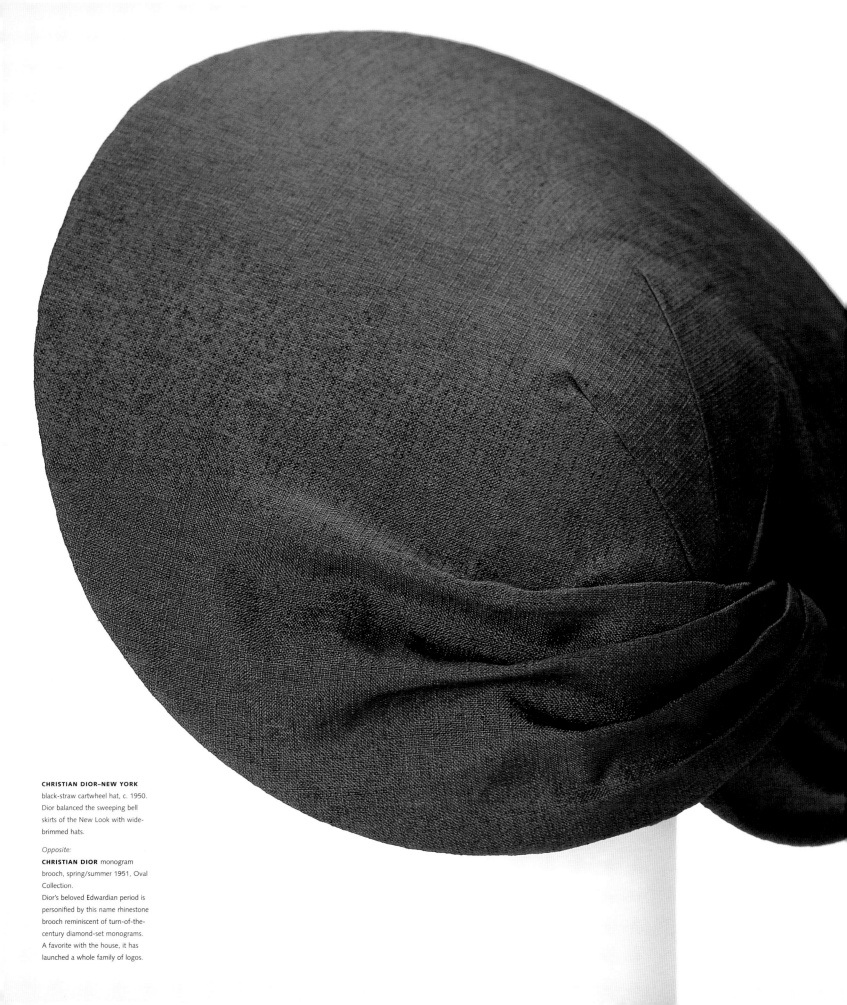

CHRISTIAN DIOR–NEW YORK
black-straw cartwheel hat, c. 1950.
Dior balanced the sweeping bell
skirts of the New Look with wide-
brimmed hats.

Opposite:
CHRISTIAN DIOR monogram
brooch, spring/summer 1951, Oval
Collection.
Dior's beloved Edwardian period is
personified by this name rhinestone
brooch reminiscent of turn-of-the-
century diamond-set monograms.
A favorite with the house, it has
launched a whole family of logos.

Christian Dior

WHEN CHRISTIAN DIOR'S NEW LOOK burst onto the
scene in 1947, it had been many decades since a fashion designer had singlehandedly changed the way women looked. As Zeitgeist a moment as Poiret's Ballets Russes–inspired
banishment of corsets had been early in the century, Dior's wide, ankle-grazing skirts and cinched-in waists
brought feminine pulchritude back with a bang, providing symbolic closure to the privations of World War II. And, as
has often been the case with mood-altering silhouettes, the new look would require new accessories. "Bar," the quintessential
New Look suit, with its pale tan fitted padded-hip jacket and full, pleated skirt, was shown by Dior with a wide-brimmed black hat, its
brim dipped rakishly, along with black gloves gathered over the wrists, just so, and curved-heel pumps. (Subsequent editorial coverage showed
the suit with a light straw hat). Suddenly, towering headgear covered with almost gaudy displays of flowers tipped forward on the brow, not to mention platform shoes, looked dreadfully passé. • Hats were so important to Christian Dior as an integral part of an ensemble that his first two collections
featured millinery designed specifically for each costume yet made by outside suppliers. In 1948, it was announced that Dior had opened a millinery department to be run by impossibly elegant Madame Germaine Bricard. Shoes for the early collections were specially designed by Perugia. Dior's nostalgic respect for
the elegance of his youth was expressed in old-fashioned accessories like muffs, trimmed with fur or ruched ribbons; handkerchiefs with deep lace borders; umbrel
las playing the role of parasols; and ropes of jewels going from one side of a neckline to the other in a bodice-decorating manner much like that of Edwardian stom-
achers. One necklace, of rhinestones, covered the shoulders like the practically ubiquitous late nineteenth-century beaded capelet. Among Dior's early costume-jewelry
suppliers was Francis Winter; Roger Model made his pocketbooks, Le Grand his gloves. • Yet the name that would become indelibly linked with that of Dior was Roger
Vivier. In 1953, it was announced that Delman had opened a shoe boutique practically next door to Dior. Here, in-house designer Vivier's inventive styles set a stan-
dard rarely matched for shoes that were like works of art in workmanship and originality. • After Christian Dior's death in 1957, his young apprentice, Yves Saint
Laurent, was named his successor. Saint Laurent for Dior was a signature all its own: elegantly fluid. Marc Bohan, summoned from Dior London to be the new couturier in 1961, had the longest reign; he left the house in 1989. Gianfranco Ferré's years at Dior (1989–96) were characterized by exuberant, somewhat classical
but always feminine extravagance. Diorisms included evening headdresses that dangled flowers and baubles, canework (borrowed from perfume packaging)
used as patterns for hats and pocketbooks, and Christian Dior's beloved houndstooth checks in black and white for everything. The variously sized letters
of the Dior monogram, first used in the 1951 rhinestone brooch shown above, began to appear on jewelry, and then, very successfully, on the Lady Dior
bag, so named when Princess Diana was seen carrying it. • In 1997, John Galliano became the head designer at Dior, and, rather than resort to
what has practically become a formula of updating archives, he has made the world, and world cultures past and present, his oyster. As
Harold Koda has observed, "Over the years, whether the references have been to *les merveilleuses* of the Directoire, courtesans
of the Belle Epoque, or sophisticates of between-the-wars café society, Galliano has consistently assimilated
the styles and sensibilities of the past into convincing contemporary glamour."

CHRISTIAN DIOR navy-tulle winged hat, c. 1950.
Although each Dior collection featured a different theme, characteristic of many of his designs was a sense of movement, with fabric flying off in one direction or another. Feathered hats taking flight mirrored this sensibility.

CHRISTIAN DIOR leaf headdress, c. 1950.
In Dior's world, hats were worn with daytime suits and dresses, softly feminine afternoon ensembles, cocktail dresses, and on up to ball gowns. This delicately foliate head covering with waxed linen leaves would have accompanied a spring suit or afternoon dress.

CHRISTIAN DIOR pointed oval brooch, autumn/winter 1950.
In this rhinestone brooch, the reference to an eye is whispered, not shouted.

ROGER VIVIER FOR CHRISTIAN DIOR satin evening shoe, c. 1955.
"Il faut souffrir à être belle." One of Roger Vivier's first designs for Christian Dior balanced on what was described at the time as a Cleopatra's needle heel. The forerunners of the stiletto, these shoes firmly ushered in a new silhouette—considerably more delicate and fragile looking than what had come before.

MARC BOHAN FOR CHRISTIAN DIOR silk coiffure hat, c. 1962. Milliners have occasionally been inspired by prevailing hairstyles when creating hats. Ironically, this example reflects the beginning of the era of "big hair," which would effectively banish the formal wearing of hats.

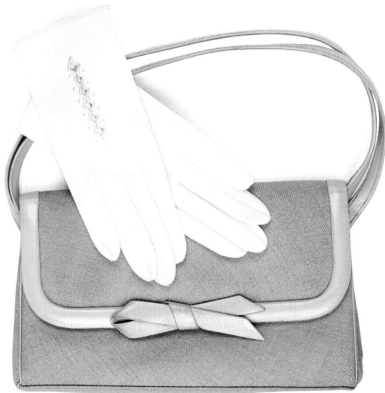

CHRISTIAN DIOR chartreuse
lacquered-straw lampshade hat,
early 1960s.
The house of Dior continued during
the 1960s to present a dignified yet
youthful look. Here a classic silhouette of the period is rendered in up-
to-the-minute chartreuse.

CHRISTIAN DIOR summer purse
and cotton gloves, c. 1960.
Even in summer, a well-dressed Dior
client wouldn't dream of leaving the
house without gloves and the appropriately ladylike pocketbook.

MARC BOHAN FOR CHRISTIAN DIOR felt day hat, early 1960s. The rows of topstitching that decorate this gently shaped hat are a signature of Marc Bohan, who took the design helm of Dior in 1961.

CHRISTIAN DIOR jeweled evening pump, c. 1968
Fashion thrives on change and, as the 1960s came to a close, the Vivier for Dior stiletto silhouette would give way to a shoe with a more substantial heel and decorations that were bolder in scale.

GIANFRANCO FERRÉ FOR CHRISTIAN DIOR rhinestone pins, early 1990s.
Under the design direction of Gianfranco Ferré (1989–96), Dior took on an opulent and intensely feminine air.

JOHN GALLIANO FOR CHRISTIAN DIOR found-object belt, Haute Couture, spring/summer 2000: "La Belle et le Clochard" (The Lady and the Tramp).
While this belt is intended as a commentary on the scavenging nature of those who live on the street, it also recalls the nineteenth-century châtelaine, a spray of objects necessary for running a household that was worn suspended from a lady's waist.

JOHN GALLIANO FOR CHRISTIAN DIOR Pocahontas-Maasai collar, Haute Couture, spring/summer 1998.
In *Extreme Beauty*, Harold Koda has referred to a "typical Galliano conflation of cultures and anachronistic juxtaposition." Here, in a single piece, his references include Queen Alexandra in chin-to-waist natural pearls, at the time the most valuable substance available; late twentieth–century neck corsets of the Dinkas in Sudan; and American Indian clothing.

STEPHEN JONES FOR JOHN GALLIANO FOR CHRISTIAN DIOR horsehair cartwheel hat, Haute Couture, autumn/winter 2000.
The sweetness and light of this Edwardian revival hat is tempered by its enormous scale and the Day-Glo brightness of the trim.

JACQUES FATH velvet hat, late
1940s.
This hat, of velvet with jutting eagle
feathers, was originally made for
legendary beauty Babe Paley.

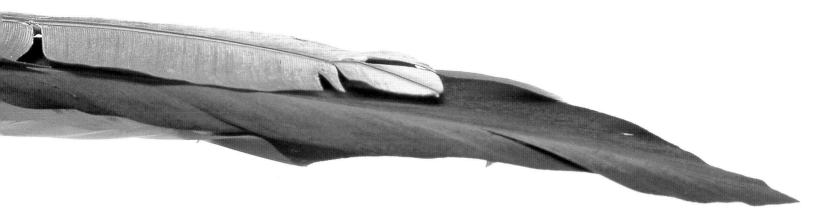

Jacques Fath

JACQUES FATH'S DESIGNS fairly bristled with swagger, with a result that was always sexy. While his colleagues of the 1940s and 1950s aimed for elegance, with accessories that provided feminine exclamation points for what was, overall, a ladylike mien, Fath's accessories simmered with energy. Evening gloves could be extra long and sport flared musketeer cuffs; necklaces were asymmetrical, veering to the side; stockings had built-in lace garters, or featured leopard prints or polka dots; the feathers on hats projected. Azzedine Alaïa once described Fath as being a "master not of cut, like Vionnet or Balenciaga, but of silhouette, which is also what makes a great hat." • The couture house featured a thriving boutique, overseen by Madame Bouleau of Fath's staff, who submitted to him designs for every kind of accessory. An early licensing arrangement, with Marvella, in 1950, featured better-than-run-of-the-mill designs. Instead of mere single, double, or triple strands of simulated pearls, Fath's designs included a faux-pearl collar, like that of a shirt, to wear with a strapless dress, Playboy bunny–style; pearl tassels, ending in teardrops, suspended saucily from a black-velvet choker; and various Gypsy-like hoops. Costume jewels for his couture collections were often attributed to Roger Scemana. Fath's stockings, (for which Scemana even made rhinestone garters) were unusually expensive due to their elaborate details and constituted quite a large business. • A March 1954 *Life* magazine spread described Fath as showing his accessories collections on models wearing black leotards in order to place his designs in high relief. The variety of amusing pieces—scarves with built-in sunglasses, straw hats with attached oversize-hoop earrings, other hats of straw braided into long pigtails—show that this was an area of growing emphasis. Sadly, Fath's death in November of that year curtailed this promisingly creative expansion.

JACQUES FATH velvet and feather
hat, c. 1950.
Fath adapted Mercury's helmet in
velvet and feathers to be worn for
tea at the Ritz.

JACQUES FATH felt hat, c. 1950.
In this hat, the expected projectile turns out to be an unexpected leaf.

JACQUES FATH pheasant–feather–trimmed hat, c. 1948.
With its up-front feather, this hat sends out a mixed message: come hither, yet keep your distance.

JACQUES FATH calfskin pumps, c. 1955.
At the same time that Roger Vivier was developing his Cleopatra, or needle-thin, heel for Dior, Jacques Fath was carving away at the toe's décolletage while keeping within the confines of the curvy, almost clunky, postwar silhouette.

JEAN PAUL GAULTIER beaded headdress, Haute Couture, spring/summer 1998.
As a boy, Gaultier loved looking through fashion-history books such as *20,000 Years of Costume*. Such a work may have inspired this Marie Antoinette vision.

Opposite:

JEAN PAUL GAULTIER cuff, autumn/winter 1986, Russe Collection.
From one of Gaultier's most powerful collections—Russe—this silver-tone metal cuff demonstrates the graphic appeal of constructivist art.

Jean Paul Gaultier

TABOO IS TO JEAN PAUL GAULTIER as a red flag is to a bull—there is hardly a one he
hasn't been drawn to. All (about his way of thinking) was revealed when he presented his
seminal spring/summer 1983 collection dedicated to Dada. The magazine *La Mode en Peinture* described the line as showing "what shouldn't be shown." Included was Gaultier's first take on a corset,
made as a long dress, a design that has launched a thousand imitations. And then there were both male and
female versions of *déshabillé*: clothes intentionally hanging open to reveal various forms of underwear. Men's
trousers were shown with the fly open and belt dangling over an insert of old-fashioned undershorts; peach
charmeuse slips dangled from more feminine styles. Accessories included a fedora with its brim slit to reveal one eye (a
reference to turning a blind eye toward, or winking approval?) and a somewhat pharmaceutical-looking glove covering just
the third finger. Whether it was the chicken or the egg, it was a collection that predicted how people would be dressing twenty
years later. • Gaultier would go on to experiment further with showing what must not be shown, including every permutation of
androgyny, fetish wear, and, particularly controversial, the chic rabbi. Perhaps most astonishing for someone who has spent his career
chipping away at perceived notions of what constitutes good taste has been his seemingly effortless mastery of the world of haute couture. • When Gaultier showed his first collection in America in 1984, his reputation had preceded him and spectators came expecting to be
shocked. What John Duka singled out for *The New York Times*, however, was Gaultier's "surprising classicism." And it is true that Gaultier's experimentation is grounded by a (very personal) vocabulary of classics. There are the ridged stripes of a tin can, first made into a cuff bracelet in
1980 and since immortalized by the designer's fragrance packaging; and the Breton sailor's jersey stripes in which he is often photographed and
which have been made into, among many other creations, a haute couture dress with striped bodice melding into wide, long skirt, interpreted—in
a sparkling tour de force—in feathers. Pinstripes and pea coats, Fair Isle and fishermen's knits, and twisted tartans are favorite fodder. High-top
sneakers have been cut apart to make sandals or added to, to create platforms. Turbans, especially the kind with Carmen Miranda topknots, recur,
along with the fez, as a hat, or, in the case of the fez, a bra. To his touristy takes on Morocco and the Orient he has added Eiffel Tower Paris.

JEAN PAUL GAULTIER hair-wrapped fan headdress, Haute Couture, autumn/winter 2001.

JEAN PAUL GAULTIER fringed patent purse, Haute Couture, autumn/winter 2001.

JEAN PAUL GAULTIER painted-metal Chinese bib necklace, Haute Couture, autumn/winter 2001.

Visions of the Orient have always provided material for couture collections; in this case Gaultier seems to be inspired not by the Ming dynasty of museums but by the more populist chinoiserie of dim sum palaces.

JEAN PAUL GAULTIER high-heeled canvas sneakers, c. 1989. Perhaps inspired by the 1960s soul song "High-Heeled Sneakers," designers as varied as Norma Kamali, Jean Paul Gaultier, and Marc Jacobs have been moved to add a heel to canvas sports shoes.

CHRISTIAN LOUBOUTIN FOR GAULTIER toe-shoe flats, 1998. For Gaultier, Louboutin made shoes with blocked toes in every conceivable style, from flats in velvet, suede, or calfskin to high heels in embroidered satin. A mere three years later, blocked toes turned up simultaneously on shoes by Gucci, Chanel, and Azzedine Alaïa.

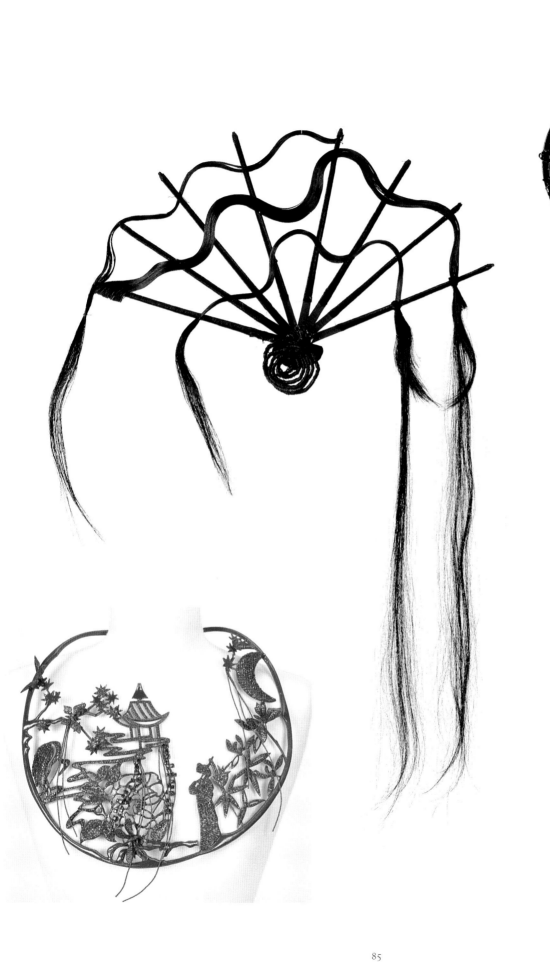

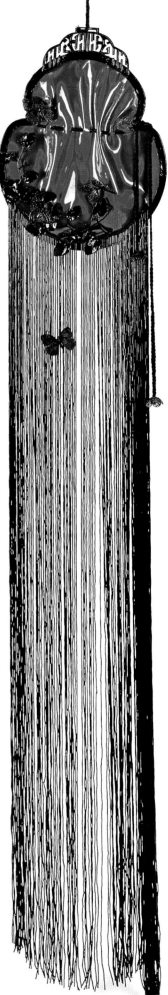

Left to right:

ROMEO GIGLI dangling earrings, spring/summer 1990.
Appropriately, Gigli fashioned these chandelier earrings from a material traditionally associated with chandeliers: gold-dusted, hand-blown Venetian glass.

ROMEO GIGLI chandelier earrings, autumn/winter 1989.
Inspiration strikes anywhere; here it is an Italian cliché—namely, the micro-mosaics found at every tourist stop—that have been refigured into charmingly antique-seeming dangling earrings.

Below:

ROMEO GIGLI knot shoes, 1989.
There's a whiff of the past in these shot-silk pumps, but as usual with Gigli, the exact reference is hard to pin down. Medieval court jester? Or suffragette?

Romeo Gigli

ROMEO GIGLI'S EARLY CAREER can be described as that of a fo-
cused dilettante. Up until the time he founded his business, when he was in his early thir-
ties, he had educated himself by traveling and collecting (along with a stint in architecture school). His is
a cultured sensibility inspired by immersion, from childhood, in his family's library of rare books and honed by travel
to all the corners of the globe. • Inspired by such treasures as the *Gazette du Bon Ton*, one of a handful of fashion publications
that can be described as a work of art, Gigli designs clothes with echoes of long ago such as swallowtail or cocoon coats,
tulip skirts, petaled collars, handkerchief hems, and high, handspan waists. The *Gazette du Bon Ton* reached its zenith in the
World War I period, a moment when fashion had one Louis-heel pump planted in a future of shorter skirts, no corset, and
bobbed hair and the other still enmeshed in a whirl of hobble skirts, silk flowers, ostrich plumes, fans, thirty-button gloves,
and court trains. Gigli's vision demonstrates the same charming schism: known for his old world sensibility, he is under-
celebrated for his experimentation with new materials, especially those with stretch. • The Gigli palette of curry and ocher,
burnished copper, red clay, concord grape, the teal that five hundred years ago was cobalt: all could come from antique tap-
estries that predate the days of chemical dyes. Techniques from other times and other places proliferate: crewelwork lace;
gilt-edged appliqués, mirror embroideries. Although early collections were presented minimally, with no accessories except
dark, flat shoes and opaque stockings, Gigli did branch out with the occasional Indian mirror-encrusted belt or head scarf,
ballet-wrapped shoe or long dangling earrings of Venetian glass baubles matching the beaded curtains of 1990 evening
dresses. In 1986, Gigli explained to *W* that he designs in reaction to the rigidity of 1960s fashion (although the 1960s are
remembered as a free-wheeling period, the dominant silhouette was a rather severe sheath cut practically the
same front and back). He also revealed his own sensibility when he said, "Maybe the ro-
manticists were closest to our modern way of thinking."

ROMEO GIGLI grommet-set belt,
c. 1990.
This belt was designed to anchor an
ensemble that combined a me-
dieval-European shaped bodice
made in an appliqué cotton reminiscent of a San Blas Islands *mola* embroidery, with a skirt of up-to-the-
moment crinkled nylon.

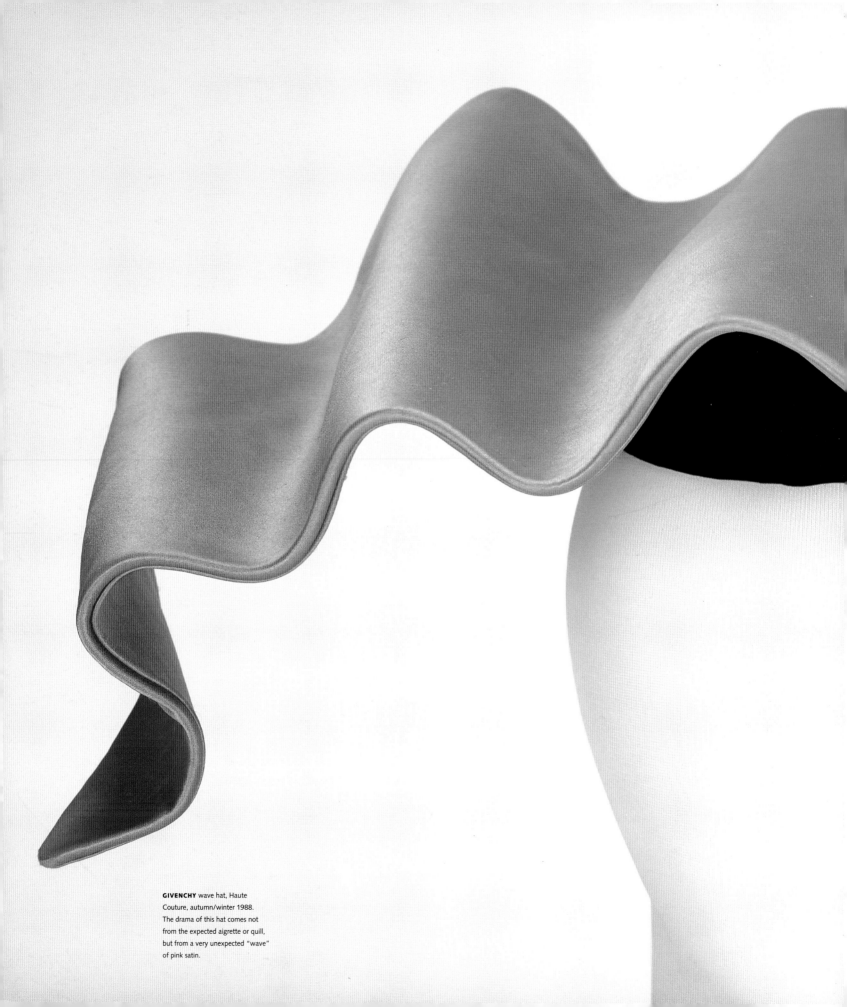

GIVENCHY wave hat, Haute
Couture, autumn/winter 1988.
The drama of this hat comes not
from the expected aigrette or quill,
but from a very unexpected "wave"
of pink satin.

Givenchy

HUBERT DE GIVENCHY'S DEBUT collection in 1952 was met with thunderous applause. The designs revealed traces of Schiaparelli, with whom he had worked for four years. Trompe l'oeil could be found on head scarves made with faux coiffures in curls or pigtails and on fabrics patterned with lifelike pea pods, ermine tails, or oyster shells, each with a pearl inside. • The year 1954 would bring two enduring influences into the designer's life. He was chosen to make the clothes Audrey Hepburn would wear in the film *Sabrina*, inaugurating one of the couture's most memorable muse/designer relationships, and he met the man who would be his greatest mentor, Balenciaga. While retaining their youthful air, Givenchy's clothes became simpler. Audrey Hepburn would tell *Vogue* that his designs were "pure . . . all line." Patterns gave way to solid colors; silhouettes began to ease away from the body. Describing an ensemble with curved cut-in sleeves, *Harper's Bazaar* wrote, "Givenchy blows air through a green suit." To accompany his flawless fashions, Givenchy showed hats that varied from simple abstracted geometric forms to freewheeling sculptures. A favorite look for cocktail and evening styles was the cache-chignon, sometimes severe, in glove kid or suede, sometimes fanciful, shaped like a flowerpot or cone sprouting silk roses. One hat style in particular was to become wildly influential, via one of fashion's typically circuitous routes. In *Jacqueline Kennedy: The White House Years*, Hamish Bowles recounts: "With his fall–winter 1959 collection Givenchy had shown domed pillbox hats—pneumatic enlargements of the original pillbox or tambourin that had been, in various incarnations, a millinery staple since the 1930s—and it was a variant on this seamless, molded shape, reinterpreted by Halston, that Jacqueline Kennedy chose to complete her inauguration-day outfit." • Other Givenchy accessories, such as made-to-match shoes by René Mancini, tended to be simple. Givenchy's couture jewelry was the height of chic, from the faux-topaz oyster brooch with two large baroque pearls peeping out by Roger Jean-Pierre to the pearls worn with clasp in front and strands dipping in back to exactly match the décolleté of Audrey Hepburn's dress in *Breakfast at Tiffany's*. • Since Hubert de Givenchy's retirement in 1995, the designers for the house have included John Galliano, Alexander McQueen, and Julien MacDonald, successively.

GIVENCHY white cotton hat, spring/summer 1968.
While hats are often referred to as architectural, rarely do they recall a building so specifically as this one does the Sydney Opera House.

GIVENCHY bowler, c. 1963.
Here the sobriety of a gentleman's bowler hat is tempered by a wreath of self straw charmingly folded gum-wrapper style.

GIVENCHY gazar evening bag, c. 1965.
This elegantly plain evening envelope is made of gazar—a light, stiff silk synonymous with both Givenchy and Balenciaga—in one of those colors redolent of the couture in its heyday: cocoa.

GIVENCHY boa, c. 1980.
Reminiscent of a lei, this lush boa is
constructed of single petals of crisp
silk sewn to a tulle foundation.

HALSTON stenciled toque, c. 1966. Halston once told *Esquire* that "making hats is tremendously good training for being a dress designer. You learn to think in three dimensions." That this toque was carefully conceived in the round is evident in its subtle asymmetry.

Halston

LIKE GABRIELLE CHANEL and Jeanne
Lanvin, Halston got his fashion start as a milliner. It was his
renowned pillbox (adapted from Givenchy) that Jacqueline Bouvier
Kennedy wore for her husband's inauguration in 1961. Designed while Halston
was at Bergdorf Goodman, the beige felt hat was more of a rounded dome than a true
pillbox. While in charge of the Bergdorf Goodman custom millinery salon, Halston crafted
some of the most outré and ornate hats ever to grace a magazine cover—which they did regularly. •
Even then, Halston's future fashion signature of flowing ease was already making itself evident in hats that
seemed effortlessly tossed on the head like scarves. Some actually were scarves, molded onto shaped hair bands.
Others were made like inflated coifs, held out from the head in what had to be a wink at women who covered their
hair-curlered heads in bandannas. There were also examples made like cashmere sweaters (complete with ribbed cuffs
on sleeves) tied around the head. These hats, or coifs, complemented the big-hair look that took over the 1960s as the
decade progressed, eventually eradicating hats (as an important component of one's ensemble) practically altogether. • With
impeccable timing, Halston switched gears to making clothes. He showed his first collection of hats-plus-clothes at Bergdorf
in 1966 and by 1968 had struck out on his own. From the beginning, his long, lean proportions were successful, and it would
be the Halston silhouette that would flavor the next decade. Floor-length cashmere sweater sets, matte-jersey long halters,
hammered-satin caftans, and tie-dyed chiffon were all worn to great effect with the jewelry designs of Elsa Peretti. A mem-
ber of Halston's inner circle, and one of his most effective models, Peretti walked down his runway wearing Halston's
clothes and her own silver creations. The pair would be one of the most felicitous matches in fashion ever. Even after
Peretti went to work as a full-time designer for Tiffany & Co. in 1974, their designs continued to be shown together. •
After the dizzying heights of the 1970s, Halston's fortunes fell. Mired in complicated business arrangements, he
fought unsuccessfully to regain control of his name. He closed Halston Originals in 1985 and died in 1990.

ELSA PERETTI FOR HALSTON
wrist cuff, c. 1971.
Together, Elsa Peretti and Halston started the 1970s off with a bang. Out with the Mod and in with the natural look. What could be more natural than an ivory cuff imitating the curves and bumps of an actual wrist?

ELSA PERETTI FOR TIFFANY & CO. belt, first designed 1969. This fluid slide of leather casually knotted through a liquid silver loop has gone on from being the quintessential accessory of the Halston era to achieve classic status. The original was inspired by a leather horse girth that Elsa Peretti discovered on a trip to Mexico in 1969.

HALSTON disco sandal, c. 1981.
Part of Halston's charmed circle (or
vice versa), Andy Warhol got his
start as a commercial artist and was
first known, at least in part, for his
whimsical renderings of shoes. In
1981, he was inspired by Halston's
shoes—including these metallic-
leather dancing sandals—to return
to this earlier subject matter in
Polaroid studies.

CHARLES JAMES
velvet cap, 1948.
This black velvet cap with satin
streamers imparts a nineteenth-
century-riding-cap quality, fitting
for a designer whose work often recalls Victorian clothes—from Worth
ball gowns to riding habits.

Charles James

ALTHOUGH CHARLES JAMES was fully capable of designing a molten spill of a bias-cut dress or a satin evening jacket puffed out with swansdown, he is best remembered for his architectural ball gowns. These were masterpieces of satin or faille, made in black and white or in semiprecious jewel tones such as peridot, pink spinel, garnet, amethyst, and aquamarine. At first glance, with their bodices built on a corset base and polonaise skirts or other nineteenth-century fashion-plate details, James's designs bear a resemblance to the creations of the great House of Worth, a favorite of the designer's mother. A closer look reveals an intricate exploration of the juxtaposition of figure-forming fit and intentionally random arrangements of fabric away from the body. The result can be "an exuberant sculpture of folds," as *Flair* magazine described the dress commissioned for its rose-themed issue in May 1950. • The handful of accessories known to have been designed by James reflect his constant quest to examine the wonders and limita-tions of geometric entities like curves and lines as they relate to the asymmetrical human form. Having begun his career in millinery in 1926, James's earliest hats were ex-periments with building wings or brims onto the cloche or riffs on the trilby. Ignoring any vagaries of fashion, he would continue to be interested in relatively small hats, often crafted in segments. James's scarves explored the limitations of fabric: jabots were made as two con-trasting-colored lappets, each sliced in half diagonally; circlets were twist-folded Möbius strips. Other accessories shared a Belle Epoque feeling with James's evening gowns; in addi-tion to matching fabric gloves were rhinestone necklaces, by Albert Weiss, that emphasized the throat, and fans made of feathered wings. • Resenting the fashion system, James retired in 1958, although he continued to refine specific designs for private clients and other designers.

Above:
CHARLES JAMES lappet, late 1940s–early 1950s.
In her exhibition catalogue *The Genius of Charles James*, curator Elizabeth Ann Coleman observed that "arcs in reverse curves" are "a major design element underlying James's work." This taffeta and satin scarf is just that: arcs of color arranged to form mirror images. Curiously, when this scarf is worn tied in a jabot it looks deceivingly conventional.

Right:
CHARLES JAMES satin candle-stand evening bag, early 1950s.
In a departure from the usual Jamesian complexity, this purse is made of simple elements: a wide tube, a flat circular bottom, a flat strip along the side, and a length of piping for a closure.

CHRISTIAN LACROIX boot sandals, Ready to Wear, spring/summer 1994.
Reminiscent of gladiator sandals, these straw and leather open-toed boots lace up with elastic bands at the back of the heel.

Christian Lacroix

THE EARLY 1980S WERE not the best of times
for the haute couture. No longer credible as a laboratory of ideas, the couture seemed increasingly ob-
solete, known merely for supplying elegant clothes
to a dwindling clientele. Onto this scene burst a designer who, having studied costume and art history,
had a curator's enthusiasm for the very fabrics and
techniques and accoutrements that make the couture
couture. As the new house designer for Jean Patou, Christian
Lacroix blew the dust off a wondrous array of cabbage roses,
ruffs, gigot sleeves, bustles, crinolines, flamenco ruffles, lush fur,
millinery veiling, embroideries, passementerie, shirrings, and
patchwork. His enthusiasm was contagious. He opened his own house
in 1987 with what became one of a handful of the century's debut collections for which the ovations seemed endless. Bernadine Morris headlined her
report in *The New York Times*: "For Lacroix, a Triumph; For Couture, a Future." •
Adding dazzle to lavishly ornamental clothes were such details as gilded branches jutting from hats or used as purse handles, Byzantine crosses suspended from black-velvet
chokers, gloves sewn with full-blown silk flowers. Ankles were wrapped in satin ribbons. Metal
that looked hand wrought, worked in rococo flourishes, brought a new look to costume jewelry.

CHRISTIAN LACROIX
large cross pendant, Haute Couture,
autumn/winter 1989.
These stones stand out from the
gold background as do faces in
Byzantine gilded mosaics.

While preparing his spring/summer 1994 couture collection, Lacroix kept a scrapbook (actually two scrapbooks), later published as *Christian Lacroix: The Diary of a Collection*. Every page is a collage of the designer's own sketches, Polaroids of dresses in progress that had been in turn drawn on or altered, and illustrations from periodicals past and present. He also incorporated works of art, antique dresses and samples of fabrics, lace, ribbons, and embroideries. Illuminating as a window onto the design process, the book also reveals how much collage itself has become a part of Lacroix's work. Linear passementeries have given way to densely layered abstract embroideries; in lieu of two-tone dots, stripes, or checks, he chooses textured patterns such as brocades, tweeds, and matelassé. Photographic images and other fragments of patterns are parts of collage-type prints. Jewels are made as collages, with various findings and elements pieced together. Hand-painted effects on body suits and ball skirts are complemented by embroideries so painterly as to impart an impasto effect. The human, artisanal touch is ever present.

CHRISTIAN LACROIX sunglasses, Haute Couture, spring/summer 1991.
Lacroix injected the couture with a heaping dose of *joie de vivre*, infusing even play clothes with glamour. A Lacroix beach ensemble could include a brilliantly gilded sun hat the size of a changing hut, sandals that lace to the knee, or sunglasses with wings of applied coral branches.

Clockwise from near right:
CHRISTIAN LACROIX for Monet cross pendant/brooch, spring/summer 1992.
Jacqueline Kennedy Onassis was photographed in 1993 wearing her gilt-metal Lacroix brooch like this one.

CHRISTIAN LACROIX heart with cross, 1989 *(above right)*.
CHRISTIAN LACROIX darkened-metal heart, 1994 *(below right)*.
CHRISTIAN LACROIX heart, 1992 *(left)*.
For more than a decade, Lacroix designed an annual Christmas brooch. Hearts were a favorite motif.

CHRISTIAN LACROIX floral brooches, spring/summer 1994 *(left)* and 1996 *(right)*.
Two handspan-size brooches typify the Lacroix exuberance.

CHRISTIAN LACROIX pirate hat,
spring/summer 1988, Luxe
Collection.
A black-velvet version of this straw
hat appeared in Lacroix's acclaimed
first couture collection under his
own name, 1987; this straw example followed in Lacroix's Luxe
Collection for spring 1988.

CHRISTIAN LACROIX evening bag, Haute Couture, autumn/winter 1990.
This trapezoidal envelope has as its inspiration the *souk*.

CHRISTIAN LACROIX evening bag, Haute Couture, autumn/winter 2000.
Here the linear quality of trapunto-quilted satin contrasts with a dense painterly embroidery of chenille, ribbon, beads, and rhinestones.

CHRISTIAN LACROIX jeweled evening bag, Haute Couture, spring/summer 2001.
For armor, this armadillo has an intricately woven coat of rhinestones, chain link, and wire.

CHRISTIAN LACROIX necklace, Haute Couture, autumn/winter 1997.
Although the dog-collar necklace is associated with the Belle Epoque, this one, with its darker palette, spiderweb feeling, and use of vintage fittings such as the rhinestone-set asps, has a Victorian air.

CHRISTIAN LACROIX black velvet stiletto-heel shoes, Haute Couture, autumn/winter 2001.
The ankle bands of these black velvet evening sandals resemble black velvet chokers.

CHRISTIAN LACROIX black stretch-satin gloves, Haute Couture, autumn/winter 2001.
Rococo meets Surrealism in these gloves painted with glittery scrolls as well as trompe l'oeil silver-glitter nails.

CHRISTIAN LACROIX ankle boots,
Ready to Wear, autumn/winter
1997.
The brown satin of these boots has
a *tabi*-sock feel, the gilt platform
sandal standing in for the traditional
Japanese platform sandal, or *geta*.

KIRSTEN WOODWARD FOR KARL LAGERFELD satin slipper-chair hat, autumn/winter 1985. In 1937, Elsa Schiaparelli showed hats in the shape of tufted Victorian ottomans. Putting a surrealist spin on eighteenth-century styles, Lagerfeld devoted his 1985 collection to the fauteuils of Louis XV and Louis XVI. The theme was also carried out in Lagerfeld-designed prints.

Opposite:
UGO CORREANI FOR KARL LAGERFELD plastic biscuit necklace, autumn/winter 1984. As Richard Martin put it in his definitive book, *Fashion and Surrealism*, "One can have one's cake and wear it, too."

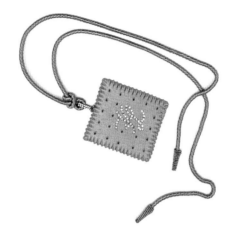

Karl Lagerfeld

Karl Lagerfeld was a freelance designer for a number of different labels—Krizia, Chloe, Fendi, and Charles Jourdan—when his work for Chloe began to stand out to such an extent that, in 1970, he became the sole designer for that company. Cited as influential were his use of year-round crepe de chine, his cheerful prints, and his mining of 1920s and 1930s moods. He had a way with appealing touches, for example his 1972 short white gloves appliquéd with playing cards. In 1979, *Vogue* touted his prescient big-shouldered, fitted silhouette, adding: "For Chloe's '78 collection, Lagerfeld accessorized everything—even the soft sweater, here with a huge prop 'jewel.' This year, it's 'fan' hats. The irony: people want his props, too." • For Lagerfeld's autumn 1983 collection (described by *Women's Wear Daily* as the best he had ever done for Chloe and the best of the Paris season), he turned his runway into a highway with Chloe stop signs. Traffic-sign arrows in rhinestones rode down the skirts of black charmeuse evening dresses. Also making headlines was his plumbing theme, for which evening dresses were embroidered with faucets spouting forth diamanté spray, and accessories included brooches shaped like wrenches and hammers and earrings made like showerheads dripping pearls and rhinestones. • In his last collection for Chloe, Karl Lagerfeld was inspired by what he called the "petites mains" of the couture. Not only were the accessories related to the tools of the trade—scissors jutting out from visors, pincushions for brooches and bracelets and hair ornaments, and threaded-needle brooches—but some of the clothes featured trompe l'oeil embroideries related to sewing as well: golden shears slashed away at black dresses, revealing swaths of red sequins in designs that encircled the body; one memorable dress was embroidered with its own mini dress, geometrically patterned in sequins and suspended from a silver embroidered hanger. Lagerfeld's first collection under his own name featured dresses described as *mille-feuilles*, after the pastry, which consisted of layers of thin silk georgette. The effect was floating, yet in a tailored way—and subtle compared to the cupcake hats and petit four and biscuit necklaces. • Prior to the late 1970s, ready-to-wear collections simply weren't talked about the way couture ones were. Karl Lagerfeld changed all that. His last several collections for Chloe were influential in terms of how the clothes were presented, how a theme united the designs, and how the accessories startled and amused. In 1984, he became Chanel's official designer for the couture and ready-to-wear lines, and, having left Chloe, showed his first collection under his own name. As fashion's greatest virtuoso, Lagerfeld's designs fuel not just Chanel and his own labels but that of Fendi as well.

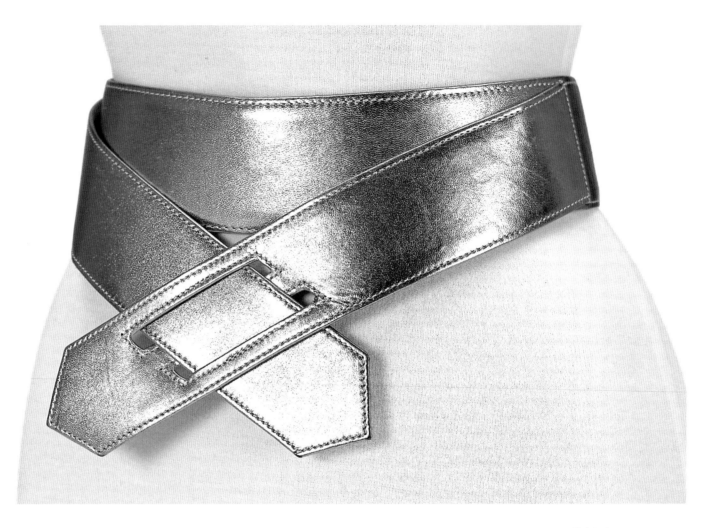

KARL LAGERFELD gold leather belt, spring/summer 1986.
When this belt appeared in Paris *Vogue* in 1986, it was described as "hyper-feminine." It was worn with a wide range of looks, from a leather bustier with tailored shorts and shirt-waist dresses to strapless print-silk cocktail dresses and evening gowns with sequined boleros.

UGO CORREANI FOR KARL LAGERFELD FOR CHLOE brooch, autumn/winter 1984.
This brooch was made in direct homage to Josef Hoffman of the Wiener Werkstätte, a school of design that Lagerfeld has returned to again and again for inspiration.

UGO CORREANI FOR KARL LAGERFELD FOR CHLOE guitar brooch, spring/summer 1983.
An electric-guitar brooch is an amusing update on an image common to both Cubist and Surrealist art.

UGO CORREANI FOR KARL LAGERFELD choker and faucet earrings, autumn/winter 1983. What could be more appropriate than faucets for a collection that made an enormous splash? The choker of this found-object parure is made from an actual shower head adorned with rhinestones and faux pearls.

KARL LAGERFELD vegetable necklace, late 1980s.
This toothsome design of gilt metal and faux pearls recalls Schiaparelli's 1938 vegetable-patch bracelet of raffia and porcelain vegetables.

UGO CORREANI FOR KARL LAGERFELD pastry necklace, autumn/winter 1984.
Lagerfeld's first collection under his own name had a sweet theme: clothes were cut with *mille-feuilles* panels and accessories were made in the shape of pastries.

UGO CORREANI FOR KARL LAGERFELD FOR CHLOE needle-and-thread brooch, spring/summer 1984.

UGO CORREANI FOR KARL LAGERFELD FOR CHLOE pincushion brooch and earrings, spring/summer 1984.

Lagerfeld's final collection for Chloe featured accessories celebrating the craft behind the couture. As the press release noted: "The belts have scissor motifs, bracelets are in the form of spools, clips are made of cloth samples, and brooches have hanging thimbles. The objects and tools of the everyday life of the 'couturier' become precious jewels."

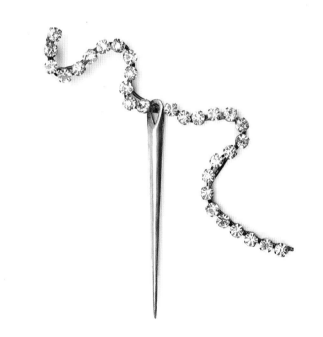

JEANNE LANVIN hat, c. 1910. .
The Ballets Russes took Paris by
storm, resulting in a stampede for
orientalist fashions. Mandatory for
the exotic look were turbans sprouting Maharajah aigrettes.

JEANNE LANVIN embroidered-silk
reticule, c. 1922–24.
Lanvin was renowned for her decorative use of embroideries. Silver
chain stitch and concentric circles,
two favorites of the couturière,
combine to form an Art Deco
pattern.

Jeanne Lanvin

JEANNE LANVIN WAS BOTH A MASTER of decorative effects, particularly embroideries, and a connoisseur of the arts, especially all the artisanal aspects of textiles. Inspiration for details such as a cluster of flowers trailing velvet ribbons, a choux-ruff of silk tulle, or topstitched kimono sleeves typically sprung from what *Vogue* in 1927 called "the most important collection of 'fashioniana' owned by any private individual." This library of documents included rare folios of period costume plates, antique brocades, and embroideries from all over the world. Lanvin was often described as an inveterate museum goer; as *Vogue* pointed out, "Her famous blue was originally inspired by the blues of Fra Angelico, and a great seasonal success was a chartreuse-green that she found in a painting by Paolo Veronese." She and her daughter, Marie-Blanche de Polignac, were both painted by Vuillard, and Paul Iribe is the author of the mother-daughter image that continues to grace the Armand-Albert-Rateau-designed black-ball bottle of My Sin perfume. Two of the rooms from Madame Lanvin's private apartment, decorated by Rateau, have been reconstituted as part of the Musée des Arts Décoratifs at the Palais du Louvre. • Having begun her career as a milliner, Lanvin was an early proponent of "le costume complét" and showed her clothes on models wearing hats and shoes and carrying umbrellas made in concert with the clothes. Despite Lanvin's reputation for an antique, feminine sensibility, it was she who, on the eve of World War II, showed (and wore) gas-mask covers (to fit either French- or British-style masks) ornamented with gilt-metal studs and made in tweed to match one's ensemble. • After Lanvin's death in 1946, subsequent designers of women's clothing at the house have included Antonio del Castillo, Jules-François Crahay, Maryll Lanvin, Claude Montana, Dominique Morlotti, and Cristina Ortiz.

JEANNE LANVIN wide-brimmed hat, c. 1910.
Lanvin got her start as a milliner at a time when most hat-making was a matter of constructing a relatively simple base or frame and decorating it. This hat is trimmed in typical winter finery, contrasting fur with silk spring flowers such as lilacs.

JEANNE LANVIN hat, c. 1920.
More than any other couturière, Lanvin is associated with the *robe de style*, a full-skirted dress that would prove an antidote to the tubular silhouette of the 1920s. Such a silhouette called for a like-minded hat: as in this taffeta version with a deep crown and wide brim. Very Lanvin-like is the trimming of cut-out printed velvet flowers and brocaded leaves, padded and trimmed with piping.

JEANNE LANVIN velvet hat and muff, early 1930s.
Another Lanvin dressmaking detail, trapunto, blown large, forms a charming hat and muff.

JEANNE LANVIN enameled-aluminum purse, c. 1925.
The Lanvin predilection for black and silver works beautifully in this Machine Age purse.

Clockwise from far left:
CLAIRE MCCARDELL elastic belt, late 1940s.
Ironically, McCardell's boldest, widest belts were designed to be worn with her most active designs: those for swim, play, or sun.

CLAIRE MCCARDELL sunglasses, summer 1955.
In 1955 these sunglasses were advertised as "bewitching sun specs," marketed as "lovely new make-up for your eyes," and offered at $5.95.

CLAIRE MCCARDELL gingham gloves, c. 1954.
Gingham, long associated as a mainstay of Americana, had much to offer McCardell. Chief among its appeals were that it was inexpensive, unpretentious, and boasted a simple graphic quality.

Claire McCardell

JUST AS THE FRENCH REVOLUTION left its imprint on the fashion of its nation, so too did the American Revolution for fashion in the newly created United States. The first requirement of true American style would be an absence of pretension—dressing simply as a form of deliberate revolt against the decadent elitism of the European courts. While layers of this attitude would fall away as subsequent generations made fortunes and sought to exhibit them, its core would survive well into the twentieth century, and there was no greater proponent of this sense of American style than Claire McCardell. Like her eighteenth-century forebears, she disdained diamonds and flash, preferring antique gold and tweeds, corduroy, gingham, and even denim. She was an American pioneer, fast-forwarded into a twentieth-century life of careers and active sports. Designing as if for herself, she dressed the new woman, often turning to the charmingly fresh calicoes, bloomers, and shirtwaists of the American homesteader past. • Beauty and function were not mutually exclusive for McCardell. So practical was she that her most successful "accessories" have to be the potholder and dust mitt attached to the housedress she called a "popover," which sold 75,000 copies of its first model. In later incarnations, the popover continued to be a best-seller, to be surpassed only decades later by Diane von Furstenberg's wrap dress. • A crux of McCardell's design and dressing philosophy was comfort and, naturally, she had strong opinons about shoes. The majority of McCardell's sportswear was shown with sandals or espadrilles, but McCardell will forever be associated with the adoption, for day and evening, city and country, of ballet slippers. Although a wardrobe of McCardell separates was shown in *Vogue* as early as 1941 with ballet slippers, her obituary in *The New York Times* noted that, in 1942, she turned to Capezio fabric ballet slippers at a time when World War II rationing had limited the availability of leather shoes. This daringly unconventional answer to rationing segued into a working relationship between Capezio and McCardell, with McCardell suggesting designs that could accompany her clothes. The resulting Capezios could be as informal as rain boots or as dressy as dark pumps ornamented with little bows. • Early McCardell accessories had a bluestocking feel to them—hand-loomed shawls, hand-knitted gloves, hoods for winter walks. Her touch would be much lighter by the 1950s, when she began making not only pieces to go with specific outfits but also lines of sunglasses, gloves, jewelry, and shoes with a breezy, cheerful look. In 1954, *Life* magazine described McCardell's foray into designing and producing accessories, crediting her with being the first reasonably priced, and American, designer to do so: "Until recently only the prosperous customers of Paris couturiers could achieve a designer's whole effect by also buying his accompanying trimmings." In creating America's first mass-market designer accessories, McCardell stayed true to her vision, not just aesthetically but philosophically as well.

ISSEY MIYAKE taffeta drawstring
purse, spring/summer 1995.
Issey Miyake's signature pleating
and crinkling are used here to form a
drawstring purse.

Issey Miyake

AMONG THE MORE IMPORTANT influences that shaped fashion in the early 1980s was the emergence of forward-looking Japanese designers, led by Issey Miyake. In 1983, *Newsweek* observed: "Clearly Miyake has found and nurtured a huge audience that most of his fellow designers have ignored. An audience that relishes the participation, the self-definition, the earthiness that his clothes allow." What Miyake introduced was not so much a specific sihouette as the lack of one. His was a whole new sense of scale, construction, layering, and texture. Oversize blocks of fabric that took shape once on the body were plays on the classically Japanese kimono/rectangle, which only becomes a coat once it is worn—the fact that the rectangle hasn't been cut into shaped pieces preserves its sense of material, and that the wearer determines how to shape it emphasizes that dressing is a process. • Miyake's sensitivity toward texture has led him to experiment with how textiles are manufactured. Although the results have been diverse, he is most known for his pleats. Following various experiments throughout the 1980s, he introduced in 1993 an affordably priced line called Pleats Please. These permanently pleated polyester materials that literally bounce back into shape can be as earthy looking as strata in a rock formation or as bright as a kindergarten chart; some are printed with artworks commissioned from emerging artists. • Fast-forwarding the kimono through the centuries and introducing new technology into fabric design resulted in Miyake's 1999 development of A-POC (A Piece of Cloth). This bolt-long piece of fabric is woven as a flat tube and scored with lines in a different texture, forming a pattern. Cut along the lines and, viola! A wardrobe of separates. The wearer/collaborator has the choice of smooth or fringed edges for pieces that can range from tank tops, long-sleeve shirts, and dresses to socks, tote bags, hats, bras, and briefs. • In his investigations of how various materials relate to the body, Miyake has made bustiers out of wire, molded plastic, and traditional Japanese bamboo lattice. He has shaded the eyes with veils of mesh, squiggles of wire, and four lenses in a row. For those who might threaten, "I'll eat my hat," his spring/summer 1994 Pleats Please collection was shown with delectable headgear made of bread and pasta.

NAOKI TAKIZAWA FOR ISSEY MIYAKE flat purse/box purse, autumn/winter 2001.
The Miyake philosophy has always included a measure of "do it yourself." This leather box purse arrives flat, to be constructed by the wearer.

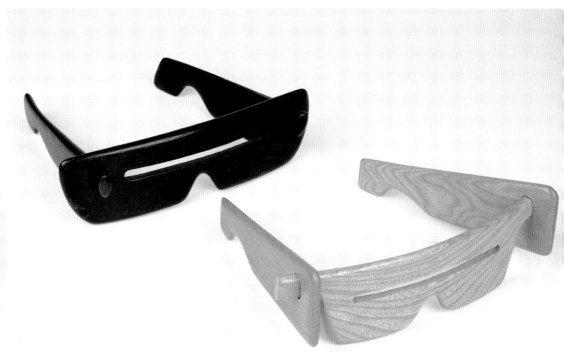

ISSEY MIYAKE taffeta drawstring purse, autumn/winter 1994. Pleating a textile transforms more than just the way it looks and feels. It also gives material a different structural aspect; sometimes a fabric becomes more buoyant and elastic. In this example, the crinkly pleating gives the purse a kind of pliable rigidity that makes it possible to stand on its own.

ISSEY MIYAKE Sahara spectacles, first shown spring/summer 1983. Miyake has made a specialty of enigmatic eye coverings, in which obfuscation rather than clarification is the order of the day. These mask-like examples, among his earliest forays into "glasses," are made of three separate pieces of flat wood that slot together.

ISSEY MIYAKE dreadlocks hat, autumn/winter 1985. Miyake's experimentation with the way textiles are made can have surprising results. In this hat, the wool was shrunk, giving it a feltlike texture. Weaving typically meshes yarns together; here, the woolen elements have become discrete.

MOSCHINO suede flat shoes,
spring/summer 1992.
Which is it? Fashion? Fashoff?
Moschino's ambivalence about the
fashion system is showing.

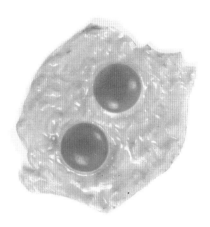

Moschino

For Franco Moschino, trained as a painter, fashion wasn't so much an art form as it was the medium in which he was driven to express himself. His ambivalence toward fashion—particularly its reliance on the latest thing as opposed to the best thing—was expressed in his constant questioning of fashion's values. The symbiotic relationship between status and fashion drove him to a cheerful subversity, expressed by embroidering "Expensive jacket" across the back of a suit and "V.I.P." in enormous letters down the front of an evening dress. In a joke worthy of Moschino himself, the great success of these playfully angry efforts at social commentary took him by surprise. • In 1990, Ben Brantley wrote in *Vanity Fair:* "Unlike such iconoclastic peers as Vivienne Westwood and Jean Paul Gaultier, who subvert traditional design with radical forms of cut and tailoring, Moschino has always shown extremely classic clothes (literal-minded copies of looks from Chanel, Saint Laurent, Hermès) adorned with surreal details (a fried-egg brooch, a clothes-hanger hat, pockets shaped like miniature jackets or handbags) which turn an outfit into a parody of itself."

That fashion itself, particularly high fashion, was one of his targets, gave Moschino's surrealism a postmodern edge. Whereas Schiaparelli had translated surrealist ideas into couture formats, Moschino, like the Dadaists, used actual found objects and turned them into clothing and accessories. A model airplane dives off a hat, a tea kettle is worn as a purse, and a whole toy-store shelf full of teddy bears forms the bodice of a dress that made the cover of *Vogue* in October 1988. • Since Moschino's untimely death at the age of forty-four, his family circle has continued the firm in the same vein. After the sale of the company to Aeffe in 1999, Rossella Jardini, who had worked with Moschino since the early days, became the creative director.

Above:
MOSCHINO double-yolk Latex brooch, spring/summer 1988. With his yolk joke, Moschino made a pun with a pin.

Opposite, clockwise from top left:
MOSCHINO heart-bib necklace; felt and bead love-letter sautoir; heart-pendant necklace; peace-symbol necklace; mirror, mirror pendant on velvet ribbon choker; black-cat and milk-bottle necklace; articulated doll necklace; bon-bon necklace with ladybug-heart pendant and matching earrings; spring/summer 1996.
In this group of jewels, all from a single collection, Moschino's playfulness has a nostalgic quality: an adult who appreciates the significance of the peace symbol might be yearning for a time of school valentines and new toys.

Clockwise from above:
MOSCHINO Napoleonic coat-hanger headdress, autumn/winter 1988.
The visual artist in Moschino recognized that a coat hanger took on a Napoleonic air when placed on the head. The runway model who wore this coat-hanger tricorn managed to look almost bored while being borne aloft on a clamshell-backed litter by two barely clad male slaves.

MOSCHINO airplane hat, spring/summer 1988.
This toy airplane can be worn arranged in a nose dive that comes amusingly close to the wearer's nose. Moschino himself described this hat with another play on words: haircraft.

MOSCHINO appliquéd-suede Kelly bag, spring/summer 1990.
Magritte meets Hermès in a marvelous conjunction of visual images.

MOSCHINO millennium pocketbook, 2000.
In addition to this lilac-velvet "gift-wrapped box," Moschino made other millennium presents, such as a pale blue example wrapped in creamy white "ribbon" instantly recognizable as from Tiffany & Co.

Poiret

Opposite:

POIRET silk-crepe wide-brimmed hat, c. 1909.
When Poiret introduced his lean, high-waisted silhouette of 1908, it was the first time (but hardly the last) that a radically new fashion would be based fairly literally on the past. The high waists and narrow skirts were Directoire in feeling, as is this crepe hat trimmed with silk flowers, which could have been worn by one of the French Revolution's *Merveilleuses*.

Above:

Minaret parasol, attributed to **POIRET**, fabric attributed to **DUFY/MARTINE**, 1914.
On April 1, 1911, Poiret established a school of decorative arts called Martine, whose young students supplied him with decorative fabrics for household and dress use. The artist Raoul Dufy was also a contributor, sometimes basing his work on Martine students' sketches. The results would reinvigorate Dufy's career. In 1914, Poiret parasols, with minaret shades such as this, made out of Martine fabrics, were available at B. Altman & Co.

THE FIRST GENIUS OF TWENTIETH-CENTURY COUTURE was Paul Poiret. In what seemed to be one fell swoop, he banished the wasp-waisted Belle Epoque silhouette and introduced an exotically modern creature dressed in his take on the Orientalist costumes of the Ballets Russes. Poiret's hallmarks were the strong, almost strident colors with which he obliterated the dulcet tones of the Edwardian period and the sinuously long, lean lines of dresses inspired by both Napoleonic and Oriental modes. Poiret's earliest styles were radically simple but would give way to lavishly artistic designs. • While Chanel is credited with being the first woman to live the modern life of the twentieth century (and designing accordingly), it is Poiret who created the contemporary idea of a couturier as wide-reaching arbiter of fashion. His specific fashion contributions aside, Poiret was the first designer to collaborate with fine artists, develop lines of fragrances, expand into interior decoration, and to be known for his lavish parties; he was also the first to lose the rights to his own name and even the first to use astrology as a basis for business decisions. • Poiret's earliest collaboration with an artist resulted, in 1908, in a limited-edition album of beautifully made prints, *Les Robes de Paul Poiret* by Paul Iribe. Iribe chose to position many of the Poiret dresses in interiors, next to pieces of antique furniture, decorative works of art, and old master paintings. The dresses are depicted in color, the backgrounds *en grisaille*. Here were new dresses, modeled after the antique but looking supple and fresh, shown as on equal footing with works of art. Practically a century later, fashion's status as a possible art form can inspire animated debate. • Among other artists Poiret worked with were Georges Lepape, Raoul Dufy, and Erté. Interested in the energy of young designers, he founded a school of textile arts, named it Martine after one of his daughters, and not only saw to it that the students' patterns, most based on nature, became actual furniture, wallpapers, rugs, and decorative-art pieces, but also used their printed fabrics in his clothes and accessories. One of the students, Madeleine Panizon, went on to become a milliner whose name, according to Yvonne

Turban, c. 1910, attributed to
POIRET.
From 1910 until well into the 1920s,
Poiret, whose fascination with the
Orient would affect not only his designs but also the spectacular fêtes
he gave, showed his dresses with
turbans. This one exemplifies many
of his signature motifs: the red is of
the vibrancy associated with him; he
was known for his use of light-
weight Liberty silks; and the button
has an almost childlike decorative
quality.

Deslandres in her book *Poiret*, "remains indissolubly linked to that of Paul Poiret during the period 1920 to 1928." Another discovery was shoemaker André Perugia, whom Poiret helped launch in business after World War I. • By the 1920s, Poiret's ideas had become outlandish and, even worse for a fashion designer, uninfluential. His pronouncements, such as his statement in 1927 that women have two legs and therefore should wear two different colors of stockings, had only amusement value. Curiously, his name had enough appeal in August 1929 to be promoted by Whiting & Davis as a designer of their new pouch-shape bags in enameled and/or sterling silver, preceding by one month an announcement of Chanel's mesh-bag-and-choker-combination designs for the same company. After the closing of Poiret's last business in 1932, he experimented with various fashion projects, painted, and held exhibitions of his paintings. He died in 1944.

POIRET pansy-trimmed hat, early 1910s.
Hats made during the 1910s, such as this one of lacquered straw trimmed with velvet pansies, could be as large as overturned fruit baskets, necessitating the longest hat pins ever made.

ANDRÉ PERUGIA FOR POIRET evening shoes, c. 1924.
Poiret "discovered" shoemaker André Perugia and helped launch his career just after World War I. This would be the first such collaboration between a fashion designer and an accessories specialist. While the shape of this pump is very much in keeping with the silhouette of its period, the decoration of delicate kid appliqué and many-colored rhinestones stands out.

GEORGES LEPAPE FOR POIRET FOR ROSINE printed-paper advertising fan, c. 1920.
Poiret's finest achievement was his response to the 1910 Léon Bakst–designed Ballets Russes production of *Scheherazade* in Paris. Poiret's narrow, gauzy silhouette, as epitomized by this Georges Lepape rendering of an odalisque clad in orientalist finery, would bring real change to fashion.

Opposite:
MADELEINE PANIZON FOR POIRET embroidered-leather hat, c.1923.
Poiret was known for adapting decorative effects from seemingly distant cultures. Made of kid leather, this close-fitting helmetlike toque is in the Egyptian style, which was all the rage following the announcement in January 1923 of the discovery of Pharaoh Tutankhamen's tomb.

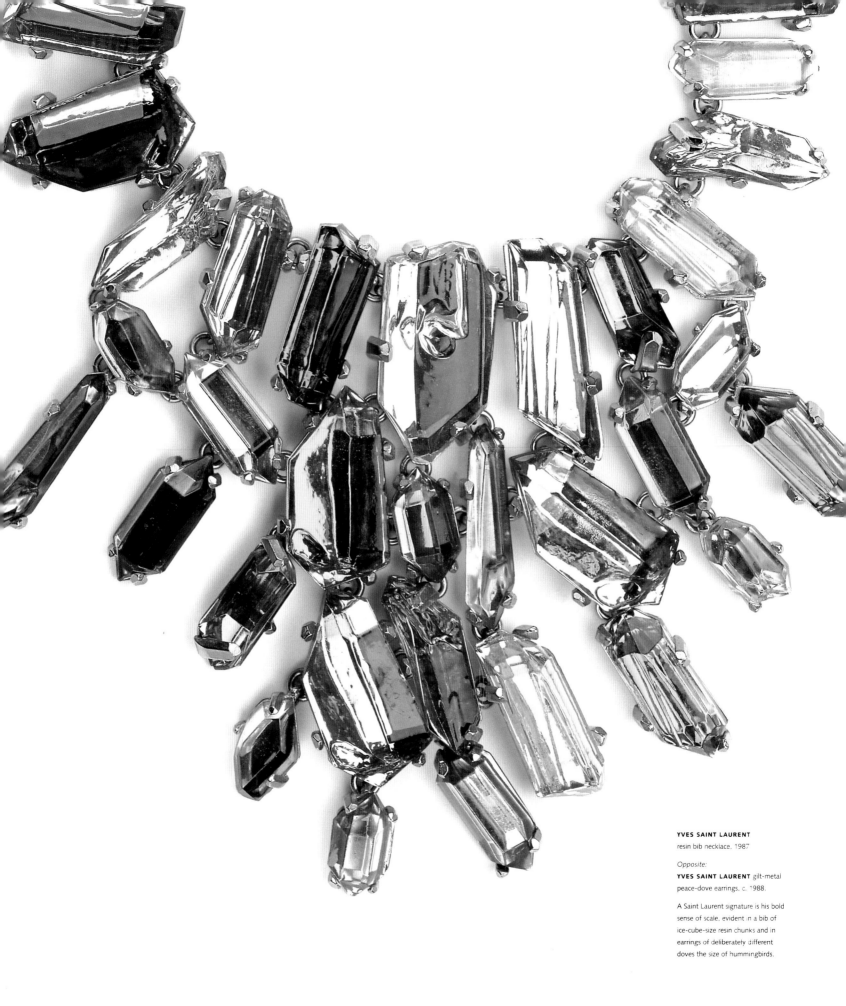

YVES SAINT LAURENT
resin bib necklace, 1987

Opposite:
YVES SAINT LAURENT gilt-metal
peace-dove earrings, c. 1988.

A Saint Laurent signature is his bold
sense of scale, evident in a bib of
ice-cube-size resin chunks and in
earrings of deliberately different
doves the size of hummingbirds.

YVES SAINT LAURENT (FRENCH, BORN ALGERIA, 1936)
HOUSE ESTABLISHED 1962

Yves Saint Laurent

In Yves Saint Laurent's very first collection under his own name, the hallmarks that would make him one of the most influential designers of his time were firmly in place. How he achieved his particular brand of relaxed ease had not so much to do with fit (as was the case in designs by Balenciaga, Givenchy, and Pierre Cardin) as with a mood that was a savvy expression of his youth. Suits were shown not with ladylike pillboxes but with what *Vogue* called cowboy hats due to their wide, slightly upturned brims; coats were based on pea jackets; tunic dresses, sashed gently, seemed less uptight than one-piece dresses. *Vogue* couldn't have been more pleased: "Most talked about was Yves St. Laurent—because of his sensational success when he designed for Dior; the general regret when he was drafted for military service; and the hope that this collection would mean new stimulus for the couture.... Most rewarding of all was the sure feeling for detail—every hat, every jewel, every glove just as it should be. And for this scarf-loving generation, there was the special surprise of the chicest babushka to date." • Paris's newest couturier would become successful for the very same street- or youth-inspired style that had gotten him into hot water as boy wonder at Christian Dior: although the ensemble has by now reached icon status, Saint Laurent's mink-trimmed crocodile "biker's" jacket and over-the-knee boots in matching skins by Roger Vivier had helped seal his fate—the 1960 collection would be his last for the venerable house. On his own, however, Saint Laurent moved surefootedly from one success to another: the Mondrian dress, a woman's version of "le smoking" jacket, the safari suit. In 1968, two moves made news. First he waved his magic wand over pants ensembles, showing a collection composed almost entirely of them (even the wedding "dress" was a tunic and trumpet-legged trousers in white and gold brocade). Mary Russell of *Women's Wear Daily* wrote: "You can compare what [Yves Saint Laurent] did with pants Thursday to what Balenciaga did with the sack, but there is one big difference. St. Laurent speaks for an entire generation. He is backed by a powerful movement of the young." Equally bold was his pronouncement that the couture and ready-to-wear were equal in his eyes, made when opening his first Rive Gauche store in the United States in September 1968: "There is no couture and no ready-to-wear. For me there are just clothes to be worn." The idea was hardly novel—couturiers had been experimenting with boutique lines for decades, and in fact Saint Laurent had designed ready-to-wear clothing for Christian

Dior—New York. What was unusual was that Saint Laurent's perfect-pitch clothes and accessories were available at all price points, without resorting to any dumbing down.

Although fashion and art often collide, Saint Laurent's knack for blending them seamlessly is unparalleled. After his Mondrian dress came a succession of looks ranging from Pop Art to tribal. Whole collections were based on the art of Picasso, Matisse, and Braque. In 1969, Saint Laurent incorporated sculptures by Claude LaLanne into his dresses, offering discrete pieces as well: *Vogue* depicted a stunning "belt" (as imposing as a corset) and brooch, life-cast in vermeil from the midriff and lips of the model Verushka.

Each of Saint Laurent's most outstanding collections—Ballets Russes, Carmen, Imperial China, Cubism, Morocco—has added specific aesthetics to his oeuvre. Thus, favorite items, such as corselette belts, ankle-wrapped and platform shoes, high-heeled boots, small shaped shoulder bags, underarm envelopes, fringed shawls, fez/pillbox hats, berets, boaters, and gauntlets, feature distinctive decorative elements, like soutache braid used as is or in passementerie; tassels in metal, braid, and/or leather; color blocking; and *sauvage* touches of snakeskin and big-game-animal spots. Other consistent signatures included a predilection for darkened metals; concentric circles, often used at the back of jewelry designs; randomly studded large faceted stones; mixing of metal with leather, cord, and wood; and large, larger, largest chokers, cuff bracelets, and earrings. Ever present was Saint Laurent's particular

balance of urbane polish and sex appeal—in see-through blouses under smoking jackets, suits shown with rhinestone ankle bracelets, or a rivière of rhinestones worn not around the neck but at the waist, to be glimpsed through the lowest possible back décolleté.

Roger Vivier, who had worked with Saint Laurent on Dior designs, continued throughout the 1960s to produce shoes and boots that particularly complemented Saint Laurent's pants turnouts. Jewelry, often designed for Saint Laurent by house muse and director of accessories Loulou de la Falaise, was created by top makers Roger Jean-Pierre, Roger Scemana, Gripoix, and Robert Goossens. Paloma Picasso's first jewelry designs, in silver, were shown with Saint Laurent clothes in 1971. Renaud Pellegrino created handbags for the house before starting out on his own. Hats accompanying the couture clothes were made in-house.

When Tom Ford took the design helm of Yves Saint Laurent's ready-to-wear, in 2000, Cathy Horyn wrote for *The New York Times:* "Nothing gave a better idea of how carefully Mr. Ford had thought out each detail, especially in relation to Saint Laurent, than the virtual absence of accessories. No hats, no gloves, no handbags. Only a small, hard purse that looked like a cross between a camera and a cigarette case." In subsequent collections, Ford has injected new life into Saint Laurent classics such as peasant blouses, corselette belts, Africana motifs, and ankle-wrapped shoes and boots. In January 2002, Saint Laurent showed his last couture collection before beginning his retirement.

YVES SAINT LAURENT heart pendant, spring/summer 1962. Shown in Yves Saint Laurent's very first collection under his own name, this heart pendant has assumed the properties of a talisman. Paired originally with a cloqué tunic dress, it has appeared in each couture collection since and is always shown with the favorite design of the season, often the grand finale, the wedding dress. For Saint Laurent's farewell couture collection in January 2002, the pendant was worn, with a black velvet suit, by the designer's mother.

YVES SAINT LAURENT faux-pearl and jet earrings, first shown spring/summer 1962. From the time of their appearance in Yves Saint Laurent's first collection, these earrings became classics. With their white pearls in black square frames, they were almost polar opposites of Chanel's white pearls set in light (gilt) circles.

YVES SAINT LAURENT fur-trimmed hat, autumn/winter 1962. Charcoal velvet in lieu of black gives this hat a subtle elegance.

YVES SAINT LAURENT hat, autumn/winter 1966. Saint Laurent is often referred to as the first couturier to be inspired by the street. Designed in a vein similar to his renowned crocodile jacket and over-the-knee boots, this studded leather hat, edged with mink, reveals a touch of the biker.

YVES SAINT LAURENT braided velvet hat, autumn/winter 1977, Imperial China Collection.
At Dior, where Yves Saint Laurent got his start, collections were based on fairly abstract themes, often given the name of a letter of the alphabet like H or Y. Saint Laurent's theme collections (Russia, Imperial China, Picasso) would plow the depths of a culture or art form for colors, textures, decorative motifs, and shapes.

Opposite:
YVES SAINT LAURENT
bead and glass bib necklace, spring/summer 1991.
Yves Saint Laurent's iconoclastic color sense is evident in this elaborate bib designed for a collection that was inspired by Léon Bakst's orientalist dance costumes.

Clockwise from top left:

ROGER VIVIER FOR YVES SAINT LAURENT pumps with Pilgrim buckles, introduced in 1965.
Roger Vivier, who had worked with Yves Saint Laurent while at Dior, designed these Pilgrim-buckle shoes, which were wildly popular for years. As part of her chillingly elegant persona in the film *Belle de Jour*, Catherine Deneuve wore the classic black-patent version.

YVES SAINT LAURENT drawstring purse, Haute Couture, autumn/winter 1988.
Yves Saint Laurent's autumn/winter couture collection, inspired by art, in particular by cubist painter Georges Braque, was a triumph. This purse of suede and gilt metal relates to evening suits and boleros embroidered by Lesage with three-dimensional bunches of grapes across the shoulders and down the sleeves.

YVES SAINT LAURENT chain belt, first shown 1967.
Another of Yves Saint Laurent's accessory designs to have staying power was this plastic and metal chain belt, which remained in fashion for years.

Left to right:

YVES SAINT LAURENT olive passementerie pocketbook, c. 1997; straw envelope with shaped flap, late 1990s; chocolate passementerie shoulder bag, spring/summer 2001. Two of these elegant handbags are made of a well-loved Yves Saint Laurent signature: passementerie cord.

Clockwise from above left:

YVES SAINT LAURENT RIVE GAUCHE rock crystal choker, autumn/winter 1988.
Since 1972, Yves Saint Laurent's frequently cited muse Loulou de la Falaise has worked with him on jewelry design. Signs of this collaboration include a heightened sense of scale and texture.

YVES SAINT LAURENT bead necklace with cross pendant, 1990s.
Evocative of mineral specimens viewed under ultraviolet light, these rocky beads are made of resin that is naturalistically textured yet fantastically tinted.

YVES SAINT LAURENT sautoir, 1970s.
A leitmotif of Saint Laurent's jewelry has been the use of natural non-precious materials like wood and, in the case of this casually knotted string sautoir, peach pits.

YVES SAINT LAURENT bead and tassel necklace, 1980s.
Here, a signature tassel is combined with subtly mottled poured-glass lozenge beads.

YVES SAINT LAURENT drop earrings, c. 1991.
Yves Saint Laurent's affinity for tribal art has often resulted in pieces that have a fusion feeling. Here, ceramic masks are combined with stones featuring the couture touch of silver lamé underlay.

YVES SAINT LAURENT necklace, Haute Couture, spring/summer 1988.
Possibly made by Gripoix, this is an updated version of the faux pearls mixed with ruby and emerald glass beads popularized by Chanel in the late 1920s and early 1930s.

Clockwise from left:

YVES SAINT LAURENT suede boots, autumn/winter, 1977, Imperial China Collection.
In a case, perhaps, of gilding the lily, these passementerie-wrapped boots were shown with ensembles of jewel-toned or metallic brocades with pagoda shoulders and lush fur trim.

YVES SAINT LAURENT fur and leather gauntlets, autumn/winter 1977, Imperial China Collection. Saint Laurent's dream of Mandarin China included opulent touches such as mink-trimmed gauntlets.

YVES SAINT LAURENT wood and gilt metal cuff with matching heart earrings, autumn/winter 1992. Hearts on fire, interpreted in wood and gilt metal.

SCHIAPARELLI parasol, c. 1935. Although Schiaparelli will forever be associated with the color shocking pink, she was also drawn to this vibrant, almost electric blue.

Schiaparelli

ELSA

SCHIAPARELLI

INVENTED THE WITTY ACCES-

SORY, with it spawning a whole new way to dress.

Her hat shaped like a shoe, gloves with blood-red nails, and circus-performer clips

were just the tip of the iceberg. In 1932, *Fortune* magazine heralded her as the "dressmaker to whom one

hears the word 'genius' applied more than any other.... The daughter of an archeologist, she is ... to dressmaking

what Léger is to painting or Le Corbusier is to architecture. She makes collars out of china, belts from strands of alu-

minum, glass rings, and coils of celluloid; [she] uses metal clasps instead of buttons. She doesn't want to make women

pretty, but often gives them a magnificent beauty in spite of herself." • Based in Paris, Schiaparelli started small—her

knitted sweaters of 1927 were a nearly instant success—and grew quickly, expanding her repertoire with each collec-

tion. Her first accessories to enter the realm of must-haves were, in 1928, fur scarves, made with one end to be slipped

through the other, and wide bracelets of matte-finish crystal disks strung on elastic. By 1930, *Harper's Bazaar* was refer-

ring to Schiaparelli as the "house of ideas." Diana Vreeland, in one of her famous columns, wrote, "Why Don't

You...order Schiaparelli's Cellophane belt with your name and telephone number written on it?" • In 1931, *Women's*

Wear Daily described the couturière as "very much interested in art and particularly in modern art." Surrealism was per-

colating in Paris during the 1920s, and Schiaparelli would not only be inspired by specific works of Surrealist art, she

would also collaborate with some of its practitioners. The dress-form bottle for her perfume Shocking was a

**JEAN SCHLUMBERGER
FOR SCHIAPARELLI** bear clip,
summer 1939.
Surrealism inspired this lapel ornament of a wild beast "civilized" by
humans and submitting to being led
around by the nose.

fashionable twist on the torso sculptures afloat in the paintings of De Chirico or
Magritte. In 1936, Schiaparelli made black gloves with red fingernails resembling the
pair of hands painted to look like gloves in Man Ray's 1935 photograph *Les Mains
Peintes*. Far and away her greatest partner in crime was Salvador Dalí—he attended her
surrealism-themed show of 1936, which included such Dalí-inspired designs as a suit
with drawers for pockets. Jean Cocteau supplied her with designs for embroideries,
André Derain, Christian Bérard, and Marcel Vertès drew up playful, figurative prints;
other artist/collaborators included Louis Aragon and François Hugo.

Schiaparelli's creative laboratory launched numerous talents. Jewelers who
worked with her early on included Marguerite Stix and Fulco di Verdura, who, in 1939,
designed a pin made like a wire-cage torso with arms and face, encasing a cube of
Shocking perfume. Some of the most famous Schiaparelli pieces ever—the ostrich clips
from the Circus collections, as well as the roller-skate and bagpipe motifs, were designed by Jean Schlumberger, whom she had discovered in 1937, and foreshadow that
jeweler's predilection for enameled figurative objects. Other jewelry was contributed by
designers/artisans Count Etienne de Beaumont, Jean Clément, Roger Scemana, and
Roger Jean-Pierre.

Wildly inventive Schiaparelli shoes were produced by a number of makers, including Bunting, Perugia, Perugia of Padova, and Roger Vivier, working in the late
1930s under the name Laird Schober. At a time when the dominant shoe was a subdued pump with a high-cut vamp and fairly thick heel, Schiaparelli showed her clothes
with unusual choices, such as ankle boots in cutaway canvas and leather for summer, or
silks for evening, felt knee-high flat boots, red leather bandage-wrapped sandals with
high heels, and platform shoes with undulating soles. According to *Women's Wear Daily*,

the success of some of these models resulted in shoes becoming a much more important part of the haute couture collections.

Naturally, Schiaparelli rarely made a simple boater, cloche, or cartwheel hat.
She liked to play with scale, particularly miniaturization, and perch hats on the brow
or tilted to one side. With brims shaped like scoops, ship's prows, or windmill blades,
every Schiaparelli hat was a marvel to behold.

For her first wartime collection (mid-season 1939), Schiaparelli's designs were
ominously practical, full of oddly placed pockets for carrying identification papers. In
lieu of a pocketbook, bracelets dangled a powder box, address book, lipstick, pencil,
and key ring. The next collections, however, were deliberately not militaristic but full of
brave pep. In 1940, *Vogue* reported on Schiaparelli's trip to New York, admiring her
black dresses and suits accessorized with jersey or fish-net turbans, to wear alone or
under fur hats; bright felt spats; and "an amusing little calendar-clip and a coiled gold
bracelet with dangling change-purse and vanity." The magazine touted Schiaparelli's
triumphant find: "a little cotton apron printed with cocktail recipes, which she bought,
at a five-and-ten, for one dime." Even today, Schiaparelli's influence extends from
tourist kiosk to haute couture.

After the war, Schiaparelli's designs were decidedly tamer, although signs of the
inventiveness of yore could be seen in a 1946 suede pocketbook and glove, both nestled
with birds, and a large rhinestone-flower earring with jutting stem from 1949, the same
year she became one of the early couturiers to feature jewelry by Coppola & Toppo. Her
couture atelier closed in 1954 and the many articles subsequently licensed under her
name—wigs, neckties, stockings, jewelry, furs, sunglasses—have none of her ultimately
inimitable chic.

SCHIAPARELLI fingernail gloves, autumn/winter 1936–37. These gloves belonged to Schiaparelli herself. Salvador Dali attended the presentation of this collection, in which he had quite a hand, inspiring the hat shaped like a shoe and suits with red-lip or bureau-drawer pockets.

SCHIAPARELLI satin newsprint purse, summer 1935. Schiaparelli's famous newsprint collage, an idea inspired by Picasso's Cubist period, was first made into sun hats shaped like—what else?— folded newspaper hats. In 2000, John Galliano made a similar collage, also featuring articles about himself; production had to stop when one of the newspapers used threatened a lawsuit.

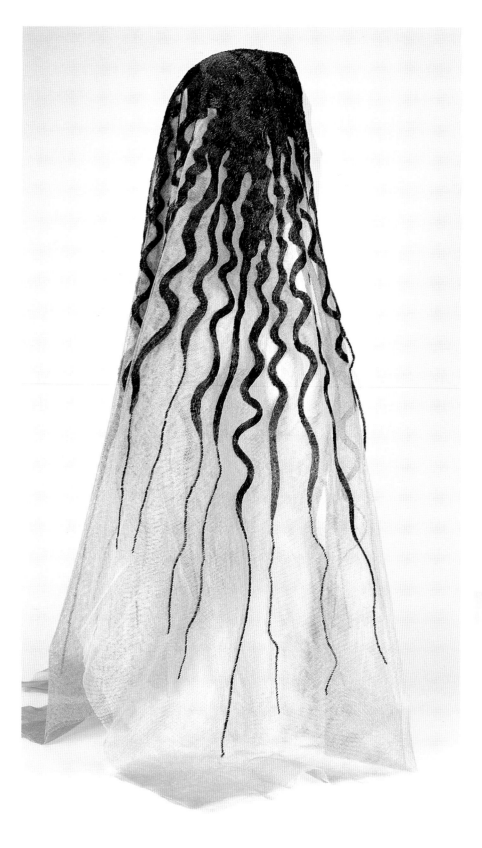

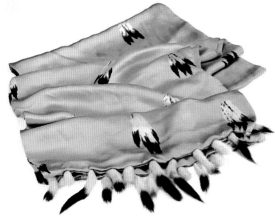

Opposite, clockwise from left:
SCHIAPARELLI bugle-bead-embroidered veil, summer 1938, Circus Collection.

Schiaparelli's first successes were sweaters knit with trompe l'oeil details like collars and neckties, and they would remain a favorite effect. This veil, with its trompe l'oeil ringlets recalling Medusa's locks, was featured in one of Diana Vreeland's "Why Don't You…" columns for *Harper's Bazaar*. The theme was weddings and Vreeland wrote: "Why Don't You… Remember that there is a distinct tendency to get away from the long train. Instead, Schiaparelli makes a gown like a First Communion dress, of dead-white cotton net, with a circular veil embroidered in points with brilliant sapphire bugles like an enormous starfish—very chic."

SCHIAPARELLI vanity case, c. 1935.
Made in the shape of an arched doorway with functioning doors and hardware, this case opens to reveal shocking pink fitted compartments for powder and other items related to maquillage.

Trompe l'oeil ermine-tail scarf, 1938, attributed to
SCHIAPARELLI.
One of Schiaparelli's most famous trompe l'oeil designs, inspired by Salvador Dalí, featured printed tears or gashes of fabric. This scarf contrasts faux ermine tails with real ones.

Clockwise from top near right:
JEAN SCHLUMBERGER FOR SCHIAPARELLI ostrich hairpin, summer 1938, Circus Collection.

SCHIAPARELLI harlequin clips, spring 1939, Commedia dell'arte Collection.

SCHIAPARELLI musical trophy gloves, autumn 1939, Music Collection.

SCHIAPARELLI enameled musical trophy clip, autumn 1939, Music Collection.

Although Schiaparelli is perhaps best remembered for her theme collections, where printed fabrics, forms of ornament, and accessories carried out a unified vision, she wasn't to present such collections until 1936–37, when her ode to Surrealism debuted, and she soon stopped them, as harbingers of war darkened the mood in Europe.

Opposite, clockwise from top left:
Brocade evening bag, 1937, Mid-season Collection, attributed to **SCHIAPARELLI**.
While the hand clasp on this evening bag is wearing the same pointed-lace cuff seen on the brooch with black rose, the roses are different. Of the hand pins that have survived there is a fair amount of variety, suggesting they were cobbled together from various findings and highlighting the fact that French couture jewelry production was far from assembly-line.

Hand brooches, 1937, Mid-season Collection, attributed to **SCHLUMBERGER FOR SCHIAPARELLI**.
According to *Women's Wear Daily*, Schiaparelli's mid-season 1937 collection featured "buttons and clips in colored luminous metal like Christmas tree ornaments, such as little hands holding flowers."

Pansy parure, autumn/winter 1937, attributed to **SCHIAPARELLI**.
While the pansy clip (*bottom left*) shown in *Harper's Bazaar* was relatively subdued, this suite, originally belonging to *Harper's Bazaar* fashion editor Diana Vreeland, featured flamboyant enameling.

SCHIAPARELLI gilt-metal pansy clip, autumn/winter 1937.
When a photograph of a costume clip like this ran in *Harper's Bazaar*, the caption mentioned "the much talked-of pansy clips to be worn with suits." While new for 1937, these flowery pieces are almost line-for-line copies, blown up by about a third, of common Edwardian jewels.

SCHIAPARELLI Victorian Revival hat, c. 1938.
Schiaparelli's 1930s work made frequent reference to Victorian fashion, beginning with bustles and leg-of-mutton sleeves and proceeding into every area of accessory, from bonnets worn tipped forward on the brow to ankle boots resembling nineteenth-century gaiters.

Bead-embroidered purse, c. 1937, attributed to **SCHIAPARELLI**.
The velvet purse may be one of a number of treatments of pansies from around 1937. At the side can be seen its unusual plastic two-tone zipper.

Opposite, clockwise from top left:

SCHIAPARELLI satin mitts, summer 1938.
While the fingerless gloves could have come straight out of a page from *Godey's Lady's Book*, their Christmas-ball buttons are pure Schiaparelli.

SCHIAPARELLI felt hat with osprey feathers, winter 1938.
Among the many materials handled imaginatively by Schiaparelli were feathers.

PERUGIA OF PADOVA FOR SCHIAPARELLI striped satin booties, winter 1939.
Although ankle boots, known as *gaiters*, were common in the nineteenth century, Schiaparelli's espousal of them, for day and night, was big news. In 1938, *Women's Wear Daily* breathlessly reported that Madame Schiaparelli wore the new booties while lunching at the Ritz.

SCHIAPARELLI taupe felt hat, autumn/winter 1937.
Its cockade and curved shape give this hat a French Revolutionary air; the winter collection of 1937 in-cluded "bonnets phrygiens," of which this is probably an example.

Silk muff, c. spring/summer 1938, attributed to **SCHIAPARELLI**. This violet-trimmed muff originally belonged to Cecil Beaton's sister, then Mrs. Arthur Conan Doyle.

SCHIAPARELLI gilt-metal pine-cone choker, spring/summer 1939. When not inspired by art, Schiaparelli was drawn to nature.

SCHIAPARELLI enameled metal necklace, c. 1937.
"Three garlands of gold leaves laid on with a lavish hand" is how *Harper's Bazaar* described this bib in 1937.

Silk and velvet evening gloves, c. spring/summer 1937, attributed to SCHIAPARELLI.
"Butterflies flutter all through Schiaparelli's collection, which is more fun than ever," opined *Women's Wear Daily* in 1937.

SCHIAPARELLI rose bib
necklace, c. 1938.
Bib necklaces were the height of
chic in the late 1930s; this one is
crafted entirely out of small painted
metal roses.

Gardening-tools necklace, c. 1939,
attributed to **SCHIAPARELLI**.
This choker of velvet ribbon and
enameled gilt metal is thought to be
by Schiaparelli, whose gardening-
related inspirations included a clip
dangling seed packets and a vegetable and raffia bracelet.

SCHIAPARELLI Astrakhan gloves
with palms of black suede, c. 1935.
Surrealism explored the tension between civilization and barbarism, a
tension also evident in these gloves.

PERUGIA FOR SCHIAPARELLI
suede and monkey-fur booties,
winter 1939.
As Dilys Blum has observed, "When
it comes to Schiaparelli and the
Surrealists, who influenced whom
isn't always clear." In this case of
the monkey-fur boots, the inspiration was probably René Magritte's
1935 painting *L'Amour Désarmé*,
depicting blond hair flowing over a
pair of women's shoes.

SCHIAPARELLI leopard-skin
booties, winter 1939.
These leopard booties were originally shown with an all-leopard ensemble: redingote-shape coat,
fedora hat, booties, and bracelet.
The same collection featured a leopard collar with emormous jeweled
pendant.

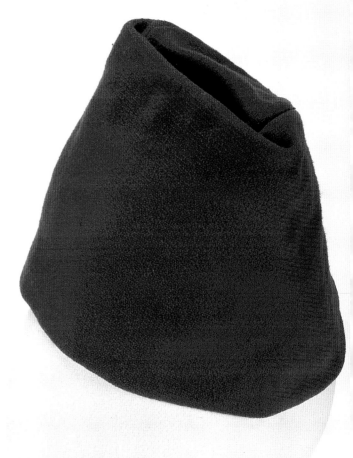

VALENTINA mustard plush-felt coolie-style hat, 1940s.

VALENTINA tomato wool twill turban-fez, c. 1944-45.

Valentina was drawn to natural colors, usually in slightly off or muted tints. This mustard-toned hat belonged originally to actress Irene Worth, the tomato-soup-colored version to Valentina herself.

Opposite page:

VALENTINA velvet drawstring purse, 1940s.
A handful of particularly stylish Hollywood actresses adored Valentina's monastically dramatic designs. Glora Swanson owned this evening bag, which has a folkloric quality.

VALENTINA fur-felt coolie hat, 1940s.
The modified coolie shape and chin tie are classic Valentina, the decoration of black braid and jet slightly more unusual. This late-day or cocktail hat was made for Lillian Gish.

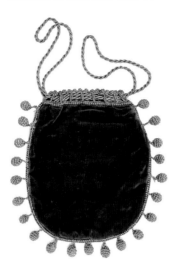

Valentina

THE NARROW, SUPPLE DESIGNS of
Valentina have often been compared to those of
Madeleine Vionnet and Madame Grès. And while there
do exist similarities, particularly of silhouette and choice of fabrics like matte-finish jerseys and crepes, Vionnet and Grès were con-
stantly inventive masters of cut and drapery, and Valentina's strength lay in
knowing the look she wanted and how to achieve it. A striking beauty, she knew the
effectiveness of simplicity. And because she designed well for beauties, her clothes were
sought after by stage and film actresses. Katharine Hepburn wore her designs in the stage version
of *The Philadelphia Story*; Greta Garbo, with whom Valentina and her husband were perplexingly intimate,
was dressed by Valentina in her image. • For Valentina, style was a matter of definite points of view, very particular tastes, and discipline. Most famous of her strong opinions was, "Mink is for football." Others included: "Jewelry
should be real"; "Flowers belong in the hair"; "Shoes should be 'light and fleet.'" She also believed that a hat must be "everything or nothing," everything meaning a "hat so terribly chic and beautiful that it forces you to its mood, or a little something that
is nothing—a cap, a hood that covers your hair and makes you sleek." Valentina's most typical hats fit into the nothing category:
a handful of jersey or wool or felt made into a hood, a modified fez, or, her lifelong favorite, the coolie hat (she referred to them in one
article as "Chinese roofs"). Because sleekness was of utmost importance to Valentina, designing her own accessories was a way of seeing to it that the line of the silhouette remained unbroken. Plain gloves matched one's ensemble. Jersey scarves served as flat hoods
alone or under hats, hiding stray hair. For an elongated line in summer, she went bare-legged; for winter, she promoted dark
hosiery, appearing in an advertisement for navy, brown, or black rayon stockings during World War II. • In Valentina's
New York Times obituary, Bernadine Morris ran a quote by the designer from the late 1940s: "'Simplicity
survives the changes of fashion. Women of chic are wearing now dresses they bought
from me in 1936. Fit the century, forget the year.'"

VALENTINO faux-coral-branch bib necklace, spring/summer 1991. Coral, especially red and especially branch coral, is a traditional Italian symbol of good luck. This necklace is from a collection that included a dramatic ensemble of narrow red draped one-shouldered tunic over narrow pants and shoes embroidered with red coral sprigs against a white sequined and beaded ground.

Valentino

WHEN VALENTINO OPENED HIS COUTURE HOUSE in Rome
in 1959, his timing was auspicious. Postwar affluence had spawned a jet set for
whom Italy was becoming a favorite playground; it didn't hurt that Rome would host the
1960 Olympics. Valentino's star began to ascend when Jacqueline Kennedy was photographed wearing his
designs, and, when she remarried in 1968, in a dress from his all-white collection, that cinched it. He would be the first
Italian couturier to become an international presence. • Coppolo & Toppo, the Italian brother-and-sister team who had made costume jewelry for Schiaparelli and other Paris-based couturiers, supplied designs to Valentino in the 1960s. Seen as newsworthy were shoul-
der-duster earrings, called "swingers" by *Women's Wear Daily*, massive beaded bracelets, effective when worn on the ankles; and bobbles
made into toe rings—just the thing for palazzo pajamas. As the 1970s began, Valentino's jewelry became more fanciful; the Italian
firm Borbonese made brooches of flower and other motifs for him. • Joan Juliet Buck wrote in *Vogue* in 1985: "The linings of
accompanying evening bags are always red. The shoes, which are designed by Valentino directly on wooden shoe forms,
have high, sexy heels. Everything is made to attract, seduce, entrance; the word 'flirt' comes to mind." Describing 1983
pumps with red and black houndstooth soles made to match a suit, *Italian Vogue* wrote, "Inimmaginabile coordinato." • Valentino is a virtuoso of the couture detail; signature touches include fine shirring à la
Jean Dessès, for whom he worked early in his career; satin used as whipstitching down a
sleeve of a dress; braided self-fabric trimming; and trapunto quilting. This attention to detail is mirrored in the rhinestone trim on a sleek evening envelope, a diamanté snake that wraps around the ankle of a
sandal, or the perfect bow on the heel of
a Valentino pump.

VALENTINO rhinestone starfish
brooch, spring/summer 1996.
Along with coral, the shells of sea
creatures have an organic allure.

VALENTINO Greek-vase brooch,
c. 1990.
Here Valentino presents antiquity,
amusingly updated and set with
rhinestones.

VALENTINO pineapple brooch,
spring/summer 1990.
This rhinestone pineapple brooch
is practically life-size and was
inspired by a Verdura citrine and
emerald pin.

VALENTINO leopard-print purse
with gilt-metal mount and chain,
c. 1991.
These feline guards suggest
Egyptian cat sculptures.

GIANNI VERSACE Pop Art print evening bag, spring/summer 1991. From one of Versace's most powerful collections, this purse features an Andy Warhol–inspired collage of Marilyn Monroe and fellow icon James Dean.

Gianni Versace

ALTHOUGH GIANNI VERSACE could make a perfectly cut pastel wool skirt suit with the best of them, he is better known for couture designs such as an embroidered bodysuit with hand-beaded fishnet tights that would not be out of place astride a circus elephant, or *the* dress held together with a handful of safety pins. In 1991, Gianni Versace told *European Travel & Life*, "Good taste, bad taste is prejudice, like racism." His was a sensibility that celebrated the appeal of vulgarity, flashiness, and rebellion. The result is a heady blend of rock 'n' roll, showgirl, punk, les nouveaux riches, Pop Art, celebrity worship, and bondage, tossed together with a little puttanesca sauce. • Among Versace's early trademarks was lavish, brightly beaded embroidery, which showed up in Maltese crosses on black shoes and on the folded-down cuffs of over-the-knee boots. Pumps with elaborately decorated heels were also typically Versace. In 1983, *Women's Wear Daily* reported: "As always the most exciting accessories in town (Milan) are by Ugo Correani. For Versace he is creating an extravagant collection of minutely detailed, heavily constructed rhinestone pieces that evoke the Forties and could easily pass for the real thing, at least on the runway." Ugo Correani's inventive work for Versace included wide belts in every shade of rhinestone; long, longer, longest earrings in dazzling mixtures of stones and links; and similarly jeweled handbag straps. Drawing on Italy's ancient past, Versace plucked Medusa masks and Greek-key fretwork to use as emblems, mixing these elements with safety pins and multiple straps for an effect that was equal parts boxing champion/gladiator/dominatrix. • After Gianni Versace was murdered in 1997, his sister, Donatella, formerly responsible for the Versus line as well as for accessories, took over the design helm. She has been heralded for the sexy glamour of her designs.

GIANNI VERSACE brooch, c. 1986. Resembling a balloon vendor's spray, this early Versace brooch has a guileless cheerfulness.

UGO CORREANI FOR GIANNI VERSACE necklace, c. 1988.
Clearly created for the runway, this masterpiece of costume jewelry craftily renders eighteenth-century style *tremblant* flowers industrial strength.

UGO CORREANI FOR GIANNI VERSACE asymmetric bib necklace, spring/summer 1991.
Typical of Versace's love of excess, the substantialness of this rhinestone choker is tempered by its asymmetry.

GIANNI VERSACE safety-pin backpack, 1994.
Has a dress ever made someone as instantly famous as it did Elizabeth Hurley when she accompanied Hugh Grant to his film premiere wearing a little black dress by Versace held together with a few strategically placed safety pins? This backpack (itself the most ubiquitous accessory of the 1990s) was designed in a punk-revival vein.

GIANNI VERSACE jewel-handled pocketbook, spring/summer 1991. This collection featured many versions of faux-crocodile purses with "jewel" (actually, glass bead) handles that mirrored the other jewelry shown, particularly earrings.

MADELEINE VIONNET evening
headdress, mid-1930s.
Only something this spectacular
could top one of Vionnet's prism-
cut white satin dresses.

Opposite:
MADELEINE VIONNET
Cubist-inspired beaded envelope,
c. 1926–29.
Vionnet's uncanny ability to circum-
navigate the female form using
geometric forms is recalled in this
purse, embroidered with a simple
arrangement of triangles interpreted
in a restrained palette of crystal,
diamanté, and silver.

Madeleine Vionnet

LIKE

CHARLES

JAMES, MADELEINE

VIONNET spent her career

honing a very specific vision of how to

clothe the female form. Yet where James might

have been most inspired by a desire to mold that form

into perfection, Vionnet's work glorified the (good) figure in

its natural state. Much has been written about her mastery of the bias

cut—the most pivotal method for achieving fluidity in cloth. Although it seems

counterintuitive, her flowing lines were highlighted by her masterful use of triangles,

hexagons, diamonds, scallops, circles, lines, squares, and chevrons. • As with her clothes,

Vionnet's accessories were closely aligned with the modernistic style that, after the 1925 Paris

Exposition Internationale des Arts Décoratifs et Industriels Modernes, came to be known as Art Deco. Vionnet

handbags (as well as her logo and perfume packaging) were designed by her art director, Boris Lacroix, and typically fea-

tured some geometric element either in terms of shape, such as cylinder, rectangle, half circle, triangle, or melon, or in how they

were ornamented, perhaps with tiered chevrons, or triangles arranged in a pattern, or even pin dots made with nail heads. A brown suede

bag of 1932, for example, cut on the bias, resulted in a slightly pouch-shape rectangle with handle. • Vionnet's sense of design was hardly limit-

ed to fashion; she was as thoughtful about the proportions of the body as she was about those of furniture and architecture. She shared this sensibility not only with Boris Lacroix, who participated in designing at least one of her houses, but also with the artist Jean Dunand. In describing the interiors in which Vionnet lived, Betty Kirke has written that much of the furniture was based on the designer's own ideas and executed, in lacquer and ironwork, by Dunand. In addition, Dunand "developed a method of painting lacquer on fine fabric, and in 1925, at the [Paris Exposition], he exhibited Vionnet scarves, hats, buckles, and handbags that incorporated this method."

Also involved with accessory design was Vionnet's husband, Dimitri Netchvolodoff, who manufactured shoes under the label Netch & Frater. In 1935, Netch sandals designed for a Vionnet black velvet tea gown were seen as noteworthy, and not just because of the design: black patent leather combined with gold fringe, medium square heel, and open toes. It wasn't until World War II's stocking shortages that it would be considered proper to appear in formal dress with bare legs; Vionnet, who didn't approve of foundation undergarments, often showed her clothes with practically nothing underneath.

Most of Vionnet's costume jewelry was, especially when compared to that of other couturiers, extremely simple. Art Deco regularity reigned. As in her clothes, color usually took a back seat to material or texture, from frosted glass and steel beads to shell and mirrors; a necklace of 1931 was described by *Vogue* as looking like gold hair.

BORIS LACROIX FOR MADELEINE VIONNET suede handbag, c. 1928.
The mathematician in Vionnet at work again, this time involved in subtraction, carving away just the right amount of rectangle on this subdued day/afternoon bag.

MADELEINE VIONNET faux-
emerald brooch, c. 1933.
This brooch provided a focal point
for a dress that was a molten spill of
green-gold satin.

MADELEINE VIONNET leather
shoes with iron heels, late 1920s.
These shoes, which button at the
back of the heel like a pair of
gloves, are supported by flower
buds of hand-forged iron. The ironwork is attributed to artist Jean
Dunand, who worked with Vionnet
in a number of capacities: his lacquer and ironwork adorned her
house and her maison de couture,
and he developed a method
of lacquering designs on fabric
used by Vionnet on all manner of
accessories.

VIVIENNE WESTWOOD
elevated satin slash shoes,
autumn/winter 1991, "Dressing
Up" Collection.
This charmingly historicist shoe, its
swollen sole so associated with
fetish wear as to be considered traditionally fetishistic, is covered with
a fabric associated with Britain's
Tudor court. Hand embroidered or
pinked slashes in one's doublet or
bodice allowed for one's finely
woven and expensively maintained
underwear to peek through, for an
effect that was both luxuriously expensive and subtly erotic.

Vivienne Westwood

RUNNING THROUGH VIVIENNE WESTWOOD'S WORK are two themes that reflect the double meaning of the phrase "the crown jewels": as sexual organs (seen in fig-leaf catsuits, penis earrings) and as symbols of the British monarchy (a coronation crown made as a soft sculpture in wool and, the mother of all status symbols, the orb as logo). Westwood's early fame—she began in 1971 as a designer with Malcolm McLaren—was as a creator of punk looks, and, as punk has proved to be far more successful as a unisex style than anything consciously designed as such, her transformation into the doyenne of corsets, bustles, and mini crinolines may seem like backpedaling. Yet she sees a direct correlation between feminist achievement and feminine display. As she told *Vogue* in 1995, "I would like to think that the avant-garde lady of fashion is not hiding her feminine power." • Although Westwood is best known for her eroticized creations—the elevated fetish shoes, corseted décolletés, bum pads—she also relentlessly explores issues relating to class distinctions. Serving as departure points are visual markers of the British caste system such as twinsets, capacious handbags, pinstripes, tweeds, tartans, and argyle. Delving deeper into hunt country (and British history) she has been inspired by the contrast between stiff-upper-lip tailoring and aristocratic licentiousness to put her own spin on sidesaddle habits or the light-refracting drapery of gowns such as those worn in family portraits by Thomas Gainsborough, Franz Xaver Winterhalter, or John Singer Sargent.

175

VIVIENNE WESTWOOD denim hat, c. 2000.
It has become increasingly difficult to "épater la bourgeoisie." This hat harkens back to the days of hippies, when rebellion was as simple as deliberately wearing jeans with frayed hems.

VIVIENNE WESTWOOD toe court shoe, autumn/winter 2000.
These shoes play with a surreal theme first developed by René Magritte in his 1935 painting *The Red Model* and first made into shoes by Pierre Cardin, whose leather man's tie oxfords of 1986 culminated in realistically molded toes and toenails.

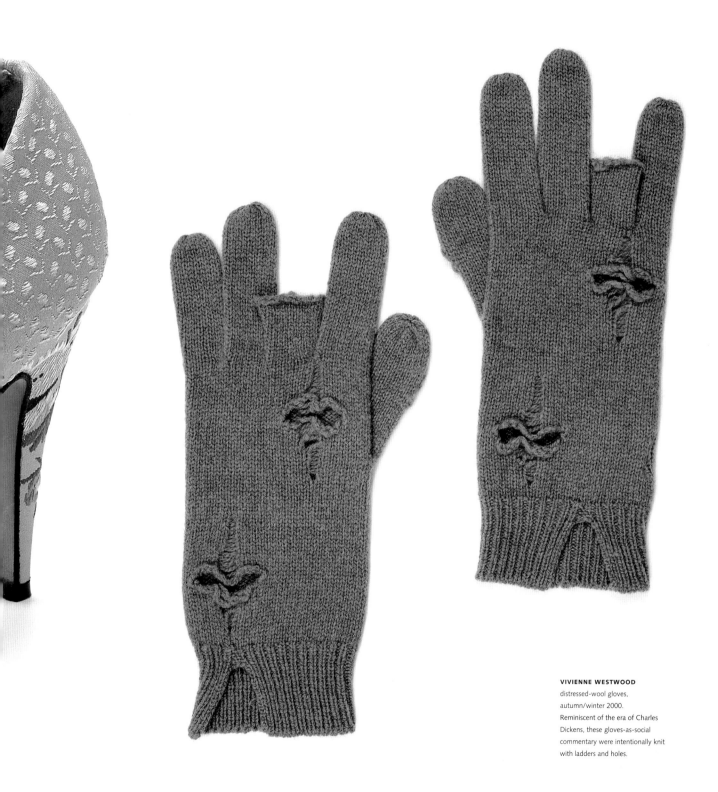

VIVIENNE WESTWOOD
distressed-wool gloves,
autumn/winter 2000.
Reminiscent of the era of Charles
Dickens, these gloves-as-social
commentary were intentionally knit
with ladders and holes.

ENDSHEETS Roger Vivier for Christian Dior evening shoe, c. 1955. Scarlet satin with stand-up umbrella flower decoration, raised spine at toe, and intricately set rhinestone-studded stiletto heel. Collection of The Museum of the City of New York 79.81 ab, Donor: Jennie Bell Whyte

PAGE 5 Claire McCardell baby ballet slippers, c. 1955. White kid lined with graph-paper-check cotton, satin ribbon ties, signed: CLAIRE MCCARDELL. Private collection

PARADIGMS OF FASHION

PAGE 8 Lanvin hat and muff, early 1930s. Cerise velvet arranged in coil; label: JEANNE LANVIN PARIS 3411 22 FAUBOURG ST. HONORÉ. Collection Mark Walsh

PAGE 9 Boué Soeurs hat, mid-1920s. Cream organdy crown self embroidered with flowers and butterflies, hat band of cloth-of-silver trimmed with synthetic silk ombré ribbon flowers; brim of changeable lilac silk taffeta; unsigned. Collection Sandy Schreier

PAGE 10 (left) Maison Virot hat, c. 1895. Purple fur felt trimmed under the brim with pink roses and velvet leaves and on top with further roses and red-purple violets; label: MAISON VIROT SOCIÉTÉ SUCCESSEUR MAISON VIROT LIMITED PARIS 12, RUE DE LA PAIX. Collection Mark Walsh

PAGE 10 (right) Lucien Lelong necklace and bracelet, 1928. Moonlight cabochons and rhinestones set in silvertone metal; both pieces signed: MADE IN FRANCE. Collection Leslie Chin. Note: For an image of this necklace and bracelet, see Women's Wear Daily, March 1, 1928, section 2, page 7.

PAGE 11 (left) Mary Quant rain-boot, c. 1967. Lemon-yellow knit overlaid with transparent vinyl, ankle boot of thicker vinyl, heel of transparent yellow plastic inset with Quant signature flower; Lightning (brand name) zippers arranged so that it can be worn as an ankle or knee boot. Museum of the City of New York, 67.73.8. Gift of J. C. Penney, Inc.

PAGE 11 (right) Courrèges boot, late 1960s. White leather with black plastic sole and stacked flat heel, cutout with self bow, velcro back closure; stamped inside: COURRÈGES PARIS, and on the sole: COURRÈGES PARIS MADE IN FRANCE. Collection Sandy Schreier

PAGE 12 (left) Lady Dior bag, first introduced in 1996. Celery lizard with gilt-metal Dior logo charms; lizard label stamped in gold: CHRISTIAN DIOR PARIS. Private collection.
An anecdote confirming the demand for this bag appeared in W, September 1996, page 80: "We knew the Lady Dior, the house's rectangular, top-handle leather bag with a quilted cane motif, was popular—after all, the Princess of Wales lugs it everywhere. But just how popular caught even Gianfranco Ferré by surprise. When he tried to order one of the $1,100 bags for a friend, Dior's departing designer was simply added to the list of 3,000 people worldwide waiting for their very own."

PAGE 12 (right) John Galliano for Dior mini "saddle" belt purse, spring/summer Prêt-à-Porter 2001. Tulle-textured leather printed with camouflage, edged with olive leather, gilt-metal C and D inset with glittery ombré purple-to-green enamel; label: CHRISTIAN DIOR PARIS. Collection Sandy Schreier

PAGE 13 Chanel purse, late 1990s. Black leather quilted in a grid, steel catch, and chainlink convertible strap; stamped: CHANEL PARIS ® MADE IN ITALY. Private collection

PAGE 13 Helmut Lang shopping bag, late 1990s. Beige satin; stamped: HELMUT LANG. Private collection

PAGE 13 Marc Jacobs apple buckle belt, spring/summer 2001. Bright green stretch nylon webbing, cream plastic apples; label: MARC JACOBS. Private collection

PAGE 14 Gallenga stenciled velvet medieval sugar-loaf helmet, late 1920s. Black silk velvet stenciled with silver and two shades of gold in a pattern of leaf garlands and flowering vines along with a central motif of stylized pinecone, inset with oval of bright spring green silk velvet, lined with straw; unsigned. Collection Sandy Schreier

PAGE 15 Zandra Rhodes evening purse, 1970, "Indian Feathers" collection. Synthetic silk satin, printed in shades of red, cerise, purple, and gray, sewn with narrow pleats, the back pleats revealing a design of narrow feathers; label: ZANDRA RHODES LONDON. Collection Margery Rubin

PAGE 15 Paco Rabanne shoulder bag, 1960s. Silvertone metal pierced discs and links; label: PACO RABANNE—PRODUCTION RICA—ITALY—MODÈLE DÉPOSÉ. Collection Mark Walsh

PAGE 15 Fortuny drawstring bag, 1930s. Silvery beige silk velvet stenciled in silver with a Middle Eastern tile pattern, round label: Mariano Fortuny. Collection Mark Walsh

PAGE 15 Pucci pocketbook, c. 1967. Cotton velvet printed in floral and geometric designs in typical bright palette, oval ring handles of bamboo-molded gilt metal; signed in the print: EMILIO; interior of purple and orange leather, with gilt-stamped signature: EMILIO PUCCI ITALY. Collection Leslie Chin

PAGE 16 Elsa Peretti for Halston teardrop pendant, c. 1972. Black leather thong with sterling silver pendant, unsigned. Collection Museum of the City of New York 86.154.27, Donor Ms. Lauren Bacall

PAGE 17 Perugia flowerpot platform sandal, late 1930s, possibly made for Schiaparelli. Black suede, some straps with white pin dots; the cutaway platform covered with black caviar beads, speckled with white beads, molded at the back into a small three-dimensional flowerpot sprouting small pastel felt flowers. Collection Leslie Chin

PAGE 17 Manolo Blahnik for John Galliano mule with wire-cage heel, autumn/winter 1995. Black silk satin with silvertone metal heel; labeled: MANOLO BLAHNIK. Collection Amy Fine Collins
Note: For images of an ankle strap version of this shoe, see Collections Gap, autumn/winter, 1995–96, page 49, shown with a floaty pale chiffon short dress with ankle-length streamers and page 52, worn with a bustle-back jacket over fishnet stockings.

PAGE 17 Roger Vivier comma-heel evening shoe, autumn/winter 1963. Geranium pink silk crepe with small rhinestone-framed cut out and self bow; stamped: ROGER VIVIER PARIS SUR MESURE. Collection Museum of the City of New York 77.98.46ab, Gift of Bernice Chrysler Garbisch
Note: A shoe like this, in wine-red, appeared in Vogue, November 15, 1963, page 138.

PAGE 17 Gripoix fish brooch, c. 1960. Gilt-metal wire, rose and turquoise pâte de verre, rhinestones, unsigned. Private collection

PAGE 17 Loulou de la Falaise for Yves Saint Laurent collar and cuff, c. 1992–1993. Gilt metal, unsigned. Collection Amy Fine Collins

PAGE 17 Judith Leiber for Geoffrey Beene minaudière, 1989. Gilt-metal modied clam-shell shape applied with red and black stones in a signature Geoffrey Beene dalmatian pattern, lined in bright gold kid; metal label: JUDITH LEIBER ©; fabric label: JUDITH LEIBER EXCLUSIVELY FOR GEOFFREY BEENE. Collection Christy Ferer

PAGE 18 Matisse portrait of Lydia Delectorskaya shoulder bag by Yves Saint Laurent, c. 1994. Black leather and rust canvas appliquéd in amethyst, teal, gray, yellow, and white, outlined with black braid; stamped: SAINT LAURENT RIVE GAUCHE MADE IN FRANCE. Collection Kendra Daniel

PAGE 19 Keith Haring for Vivienne Westwood radiant baby brooches, autumn/winter, 1983. Black-painted copper and brass, unsigned. Collection Louise Doktor
Note: For a photograph of Vivienne Westwood wearing a jersey cardigan pinned together with brooches like these, see Gene Krell, Vivienne Westwood (Paris: Universe/Vendome, 1997), 37.
Note: For an illustration of brooches like these worn on the runway on the lapel of a toggle-fastened jacket, see British Vogue, August 1983, page 98.

PAGE 19 Stephen Sprouse "Back Words" Graffiti stockings, 1985. Hot pink printed with backwards words in black. Collection Holly Brubach

PAGE 19 Chanel Pop Art purse, autumn/winter 2001. Printed leather and patent leather; signed: CHANEL MADE IN ITALY. Collection Sandy Schreier
Note: For an image of this purse, see Elle, August 2001, page 197.

PAGE 19 Sybilla cube purse, late 1980s. Brown leather, unsigned. Collection Holly Brubach

PAGE 21 John Galliano for Christian Dior pig-mask hat, Haute Couture; spring/summer 1999 Collection Cocteau. Hand-painted papier-mâché, black satin ribbon; label: CHRISTIAN DIOR PARIS MADE IN FRANCE. Collection Mark Walsh
Note: For a runway image of this hat, worn with a fitted white dress

with asymmetric collar, see www.firstVIEW.com, Haute Couture spring 1999/Christian Dior, image 67 out of 114.

PAGE 21 Ugo Correani for Karl Lagerfeld chair brooches, autumn/winter 1985. Gold-painted composition, with blue or amber rhinestone seats; signed: U. CORREANI. Collection Karen Davidov

PAGE 21 Schiaparelli phone-dial compact, mid-season collection 1935. Enameled silvertone metal and celluloid (for the numbered panel); one of the circles marked: DÉPOSÉ TOUS PAYS; the interior marked: MODÈLE DÉPOSÉ, MADE IN FRANCE. Collection Leslie Chin
Note: For images of phone dial compacts, see Women's Wear Daily, April 30, 1935, page 33, and Harper's Bazaar, October 1935, page 175.

PAGE 21 Moschino Napoleonic coat-hanger headdress, autumn/winter 1988. Fur coat hanger mounted on a taffeta-covered headband; the hanger labeled: MOSCHINO FUR FOR FUN, with signature red heart. Collection Moschino
Note: For an image of this headdress as shown in the runway tableau, see X Anni di Kaos! 1983–1993, Franco Moschino and Lida Castelli, eds. (Milan: Edizioni Lybra Immagine, 1993). See also British Vogue, September 1988, page 303.

PAGE 21 John Galliano for Christian Dior Surrealist-eye brooch, spring/summer 1999. Silvertone metal set with rhinestones, enameled face with roman numerals, rhinestones teardrop in one corner; metal label: CHRISTIAN DIOR BOUTIQUE ®.
Note: For an image of this brooch as worn on the runway, see www.firstVIEW.com/Haute Couture spring 1999/Christian Dior, image 64 of 114, and Collezioni, Haute Couture spring/summer 1999, page 191.

PAGE 22 Christian Lacroix large cross pin, Haute Couture, autumn/winter 1988. Gilt-metal dangling faux baroque pearls set with pale pink stones; marked: CL MONOGRAM with an asterisk. Collection Christian Lacroix

PAGE 23 Karl Lagerfeld fan purse, 1980s. Black faille and gilt metal, small functional pocket on exterior; metal label: KARL LAGERFELD PARIS MADE IN FRANCE.

Collection Sandy Schreier
Note: This purse is a practically verbatim version of a 1940s example.

PAGE 23 Bonnie Cashin for Crescendoe glove with ornamental turnscrew, c. 1969–73. Golden-ocher suede with brass closure, unsigned. Collection Museum of the City of New York 92.36.2ab, Donor Bonnie Cashin
"The brass toggle closures that became [Cashin's] signature were inspired by the fasteners on her car's rag top." Amy M. Spindler, "Design for Living," The New York Times Magazine, January 7, 2001, page 43.

PAGE 23 Gripoix for Christian Dior lily-of-the-valley brooch, mid-20th century. Brass wire, green pâte de verre, slightly baroque faux pearl pendants with pâte de verre caps; signed: FRANCE. Collection Leslie Chin

PAGE 23 Yves Saint Laurent peace-dove earrings, c. 1988. Gilt metal; marked: YSL. Collection Kendra Daniel

PAGE 23 Versace Medusa pocketbook, 1992. Black calf with gilt Medusa face surrounded by Greek-key style fretwork, black cord strap; label: GIANNI VERSACE COUTURE. Collection Marina Schiano

PAGE 23 Vivienne Westwood orb and crossbones brooch, c. 2001. Silvertone metal set with rhinestones; signed: VIVIENNE WESTWOOD. Private collection

PAGE 23 Chanel silhouette earrings, 1990s. Hammered gilt metal enameled in black with an image of Mademoiselle Chanel striking a classic pose, edged with faux pearls; signed: CHANEL 2 CC 4 MADE IN FRANCE. Collection Sandy Schreier

PAGE 23 Patrick Kelly "button" earrings, Homage to Chanel Collection, autumn/winter 1988. Black plastic buttons set in gilt metal, signed: Patrick Kelly Paris Made in France. Private collection

PAGE 25 Rifat Ozbek neck corset, 1995. White synthetic satin sewn with iridescent rhinestones; label: MICHELE MONTAGNE—184 RUE SAINT-MAUR—75010 PARIS—TEL. 01/42 03 91 00—FAX. 01/ 42 03 12 22. Collection Louise Doktor
Note: Similar neck corsets appeared in Mirabella, February 1995, page 125.

PAGE 25 Martin Margiella tabi boot, c. 1990. Black leather, fas-

tened at the back with smooth silvertone metal tabs; labeled: MADE IN ITALY and VERRO CUIR. Collection Cara Friemann

PAGE 25 Ugo Correani for Karl Lagerfeld for Chloë screw earrings, autumn/winter 1983. Gray metal with faux pearl drops, unsigned. Collection Louise Doktor

PAGE 25 Sonia Rykiel bra necklace, autumn/winter 1998. Faceted red, clear and silver beads, unsigned. Collection Ella Milbank Foshay
Note: For a Mario Testino photograph of a model wearing a necklace like this one, see L'Officiel, August 1998, page 15.

PAGE 26 Stephen Jones for John Galliano for Dior red corset top hat, Haute Couture, autumn/winter 2000, The Wedding Collection. Cranberry satin and lace, with lace crown, the interior circular panel machine embroidered with a CD, and edged with white lace woven with the name Dior and a canework pattern; label: CHRISTIAN DIOR MADE IN FRANCE. Collection Mark Walsh
Note: For a runway image of this hat, worn with a curvaceous red lace and silk ensemble, bisected by zippers, see www.firstVIEW.com, Haute Couture fall 2000/Christian Dior, image 135 out of 144.

PAGE 27 Geoffrey Beene shirt-sleeves scarf, autumn/winter 1994. Gray pinstriped silk taffeta, unsigned. Collection Geoffrey Beene

PAGE 27 Commes des Garçons flower-appliqué oxford, 1990s. Leather printed in black and white gingham appliquéd with black and red flowers, labeled; COMMES DES GARÇONS MADE IN JAPAN. Collection Sandy Schreier

PAGE 27 Diego della Valle for Geoffrey Beene man's dancing pump, autumn/winter 1988. Black calf, suede, and patent leather with bow of frill-edged taffeta ribbon; marked: BEENE BAG MADE IN ITALY. Collection Geoffrey Beene
Note: For an image of shoes like these, shown with a three piece outfit of lace-trimmed leather bolero, lace T-shirt, and wool jersey trousers, see New York Woman, September 1988, page 122.

ADRIAN
Geoffrey Beene on Adrian's salon: "very Grecian . . .": From an interview with Geoffrey Beene and Jane Trapnell Marino, June 26, 2000.

PAGE 28 Platform sandal, early 1940's. Robin Hood green suede; label: AN ADRIAN ORIGINAL EXCLUSIVELY FOR GOLD'S. Collection Mark Walsh

PAGE 30 Beet root-trimmed hat, spring/summer 1942. Deep beet red lacquered straw catwheel decorated with feather beets, the feather beet tops with hand-painted veins; labels: ADRIAN ORIGINAL and BONWIT TELLER, Fifth Avenue, New York. Collection Mark Walsh
Note: A hat like this appeared in a Town & Country ad in Harper's Bazaar, March 1, 1942, page 10. It was worn tilted over one ear, with a light colored wool suit with classically Adrian broad shoulders and narrow, below the knee length skirt.

PAGE 30 Feathered headpiece, early 1940s. Black plush covered with coq feathers; label: ADRIAN ORIGINAL. Collection Mark Walsh

PAGE 30 Coq-plume toque, early 1940s. Deep purple-blue felt with feathers flowing forth from the opening; label: ADRIAN CUSTOM. Collection Sandy Schreier

PAGE 31 Wide-brimmed hat with sugar loaf crown, c. 1945. Burnt sugar natural straw with matching grosgrain ribbon hatband; label: ADRIAN ORIGINAL. Collection Sandy Schreier

AZZEDINE ALAÏA
". . . power that might . . .": Women's Wear Daily, November 23, 1981, page 10.

PAGE 32 White calf-skirt belt, early 1990s. White calf with fringes ending in white or cream florets centered with silvertone metal studs; stamped: ALAÏA PARIS MADE IN FRANCE. Collection Sandy Schreier

PAGE 33 Eyelet belt, spring/summer 1992. Black leather, with metal buckles. Collection Azzedine Alaïa. Photograph by Jérôme Schlomoff

PAGE 34 Azzedine Alaïa for Louis Vuitton Centennial pocketbook, 1996. Leopard-stenciled hair calf and monogram toile, the interior items including zippered purse with monogram on one side, leopard on the other; lipstick case; compact case with gilt-metal compact; comb case; and condom case. Private collection

PAGE 35 Plexiglass shoe, jambe Naomi, spring/summer 1992. Collection Azzedine Alaïa. Photograph by Jérôme Schlomoff

PAGE 35 Platform open-toe espadrilles, summer 1991. Rose pink and white Tati-striped cotton denim; label: ALAÏA CUIR VERITABLE FABRIQUE EN ITALIE DOUBLE PEAU DÉSSUS PEAU. Collection Titi Halle
Note: For a photograph of Naomi Campbell dressed in a Tati check hot pants, bra, beret, and gloves ensemble along with shoes in this style, see Alaïa, (Göttingen, Germany: Steidl Publishers, 1998) 174–175 (photographs by Ellen von Unwerth originally taken for Interview June 1991). See also a sketch by Thierry Perez of Naomi Campbell wearing Tati bustier, leggings, mules, and handbag in: Elle, March 1991, page 228; see Vogue, May 1991, page 228, for a photograph of Christy Turlington wearing visor cap, long gloves, sleeveless top, hot pants and platform sandals, all in this print.

ARMANI
" . . .the Milan sensation.": Vogue, January 1978, page 119.

PAGE 37 Scarf necklace, c.1994. Darkened chain link mesh with black faceted beads and tassels; unsigned. Collection Giorgio Armani

PAGE 38 Choker, 1998. Small clear glass beads, pale green beads and beige nylon horsehair suspending large rutilated quartz pendant, unsigned. Private collection

PAGE 38 Coiled cord earrings, 1994. Swirly plastic-bead ear clips dangling coiled beige cord circles embroidered with dimpled copper beads; metal tag imprinted: GIORGIO ARMANI. Collection Sandy Schreier

PAGE 38 Glove, autumn/winter 1992. Black satin with white satin cuff, unsigned. Collection Giorgio Armani
Note: For an image of the dress for which these gloves were made, see an ad that appeared in Avenue, November 1992, as well as in Tatler, October 1992, page 134.

PAGE 39 Flat shoe, c. 1984. Clear plastic, black velvet; label: GIORGIO ARMANI MADE IN ITALY. Collection Giorgio Armani

PAGE 39 Bracelet, c. 1990. Knotted gray silk cord and beaded cord; unsigned, paper tag: GIORGIO ARMANI. Collection Amelie Rives Rennolds

PAGE 39 Suite of accessories, spring/summer 1993: White raffia cap, no label. Beige-on-beige

embroidered fabric flat slingback mary janes; label: GIORGIO ARMANI MADE IN ITALY. Embroidered evening bag with wrist strap; metal tag: GIORGIO ARMANI. White cord and passementerie tasseled belt Drop earrings of silvertone metal with pearlized beads, unsigned. Collection Giorgio Armani
Note: For a photograph showing this cap, belt and purse, as worn with an ivory silk two piece dress with strapless tucked bodice, see Giorgio Armani (New York: Guggenheim Museum, 2000), page 322, catalogue entry 139. For a runway photo of the ensemble, see W, November 23–30, 1992.

BALENCIAGA
"Balenciaga does pearls...": Harper's Bazaar, September 1938, page 70.
"...once in a lifetime...": Vogue, December 1947.
"I count half-a-dozen...": Célia Bertin, Paris à la Mode A Voyage of Discovery, Marjorie Deans, trans., Marial Deans, illus. (London: Victor Gollancz, Ltd., 1956), 228.
"...jet heart-throb of a clip...": Vogue, April 15, 1961.
"...the man who...": The New York Times, 1967, August 4, page 67.

PAGE 40 Navy stripped-feather spiral pillbox hat, early 1950s. Navy tulle-lined small pillbox sewn with navy stripped feathers, the feather spines sewn to the hat, beginning in the center of the top, in a dense spiral extending to the edges; label: BALENCIAGA 10, AVENUE GEORGES V, PARIS. Provenance: Mrs. Harvey S. Firestone Jr. Collection Sandy Schreier

PAGE 41 Robert Goossens for Balenciaga necklace, 1960s. Gilt-metal findings strung on snake chain set with teardrop and round rhinestones; signed plaque: BALENCIAGA. Provenance: Robert Goossens archives. Collection Tian Dayton

PAGE 42 Robert Goossens for Balenciaga brooch, 1960s. Gilt-metal bead wire frame, wired with red faceted beads and silvertone metal and rhinestone rondels surmounted by a bezel-set green pâte de verre stone; stamped: BALENCIAGA. Provenance: Robert Goossens archives. Private collection

PAGE 42 René Schnerb for Balenciaga medallion evening bag, 1939. Brass inset with a band of rose velvet (nap worn away), the

interior filled with yellow satin pockets, unsigned. Collection Karen Davidov
Note: For a sketch of a piece like this, see *Vogue*, September 1, 1939, page 54.

PAGE 43 Lead pony hat, 1953. Pale blush pink silk satin, the foundation of tulle over straw, the tuft ending in self-fringed edges; label: BALENCIAGA 10, AVENUE GEORGES V, PARIS. Collection Sandy Schreier
Note: A similar hat, photographed by John Rawlings, and modeled by Suzy Parker, appeared in Marie-Andrée Jouve and Jacqueline Demornex, *Balenciaga* (New York: Rizzoli, 1989), 295. The same photograph appears in the catalogue published in connection with the 1985–86 exhibition at the Musée Historique des Tissus, Lyons: Homage à Balenciaga, (Paris: Éditions Herscher, 1985) page 102, (Photo John Rawlings courtesy *Vogue* London).

PAGE 44 Evening purse, 1950s. Dark ruby silk satin, narrowly pleated; gilt-stamp: BALENCIAGA PARIS. Provenance: Ruth Gordon. Collection Sandy Schreier

PAGE 45 Attributed to Balenciaga, autumn/winter 1951. Cocktail hat of black velvet with pale pink rose and white curly ostrich; label: MADE TO ORDER HAT BERGDORF GOODMAN FIFTH AVE. AT 58TH ST., model number: 9758. Private collection
Note: In addition to off-the-rack and made-to-order hats, Bergdorf's sold original French models, of which this is one. Balenciaga was a favorite designer, and the department purchased fifteen original models there every season.

PAGE 45 White tulle *mille-feuilles hat*, spring/summer 1964; label: BALENCIAGA 10, AVENUE GEORGES, PARIS. Philadelphia Museum of Art, Purchased with funds contributed by Mrs. Howard H. Lewis 1993.51.2a

PAGE 45 Curry plush hat with black ostrich feathers, autumn/winter 1950; label: BALENCIAGA 10 AVENUE GEORGES V PARIS MADE IN FRANCE. Provenance: Babe Paley. Collection Mark Walsh
Note: A similar hat, in bright blue, with a wider brim, was photographed on Babe Paley (then Mrs. Cushing Mortimer) by Erwin Blumenfield for *Vogue*, February 1947, pages 162–163.
A smaller version was photographed in October 1950 by Irving Penn—and appears in *Homage à Balenciaga*, (Paris: Éditions Herscher, 1985), 49 (catalogue published in connection with the 1985–1986 exhibition at the Musée Historique des Tissus, Lyons), and also Marie-Andrée Jouve and Jacqueline Demornex, *Balenciaga* (New York: Rizzoli, 1989).

PAGE 45 Curly ostrich hat, autumn/winter 1962. White curly ostrich over a pillbox base of pale robin's egg blue silk, black silk satin ribbon bow; label: BALENCIAGA 10, AVENUE GEORGE V, PARIS. Collection Philadelphia Museum of Art, Gift of Mr. and Mrs. Rodolphe Meyer de Schauensee 1978.156.26

GEOFFREY BEENE

page 46 Horsehair necklace/boa, autumn/winter 2000. Red horsehair with aluminum-tube-bead tips, unsigned. Collection Geoffrey Beene

PAGE 47 Neoprene cuff, spring/summer 1998. Cuff of white neoprene, fastening with black and white buttons; labeled: GEOFFREY BEENE. Courtesy Geoffrey Beene

PAGE 48 Plastic bracelet, autumn/winter 1997. Clear plastic tubing with flower of large black oval plastic disks, unsigned. Collection Geoffrey Beene

PAGE 48 Lucite necklace, autumn/winter 1999. Black-edged clear Lucite disks strung on black tubing, unsigned. Collection Geoffrey Beene

PAGE 48 Rubber and plastic necklace, autumn/winter 1999. Black rubber tubing with neon-yellow spike beads, unsigned. Collection Geoffrey Beene

PAGE 48 Neoprene collar, autumn/winter 1997. Collar of pierced black neoprene disks strung on black rubber tubing, unsigned. Collection Geoffrey Beene

PAGE 49 Scrunchie bracelet, autumn/winter 1998. Brown/gray patterned velvet sewn with tortoise stripe paillettes, unsigned. Collection Geoffrey Beene

PAGE 49 Scrunchie bracelet, autumn/winter 1998. Silver/black fabric sewn with sequins and silver ball and tassel, unsigned. Collection Geoffrey Beene

PAGE 50 Satin and wool long gloves, autumn/winter 1990. Long gloves of black wool knit inset with dark green satin, unsigned. Collection Geoffrey Beene

PAGE 50 Embroidered jersey glove, spring/summer 1994. Turquoise jersey embroidered in hot pink with Flora motif, unsigned. Collection Geoffrey Beene
Note: A glove like this was photographed for *The New York Times*, November 5, 1993, page B10.

PAGE 50 Zipper gloves, spring/summer 1999. Black stretch satin with green or yellow metallic zippers, unsigned. Collection Geoffrey Beene

page 50 Handkerchief cuff glove, spring/summer 1987. Black cotton, black-and-white checked cotton. Collection Geoffrey Beene
Note: Gloves like this, in white with striped cotton ties, appeared in *Elle*, January 1987, page 113.

PAGE 51 Shaped belt, spring/summer 1988. Yellow silk gazar top-stitched in red; label: GEOFFREY BEENE NEW YORK. Collection Geoffrey Beene

PAGE 51 Shaped belt, autumn/winter 1995. Haired calf stenciled in a brown/white houndstooth pattern, unsigned. Collection Geoffrey Beene

PAGE 51 Harness/belt, autumn/winter 1998. Black tulle and narrow tape bands, unsigned. Collection Geoffrey Beene
"...overlay, segment, and define...": The Metropolitan Museum of Art *Bulletin*, Fall 2001, page 69

CARDIN

"...flaking all over...": *Time*, December 23, 1974, page 18.

PAGE 52 Hat, c. 1966. Marine-blue fur felt in the shape of an ancient helmet; label: CREATION PIERRE CARDIN PARIS; the interior also sewn with a small three leaf braid motif with tassel. Philadelphia Museum of Art, purchased with funds contributed by an anonymous donor 1993.51.1

PAGE 53 Ring, c. 1970. 14K gold, sterling silver and carnelian; signed: PIERRE CARDIN PARIS–NEW YORK STERLING SILVER ARGENT 14K. Collection Sandy Schreier

PAGE 54 Three evening bags, 1970. Faceted metal and/or glass beads, gilt-metal frames, clasps engraved or molded in the shape of the monogram PC; labels: PIERRE CARDIN PARIS. Collection Mark Walsh and private collection
Note: For an image of beaded bags similar to these, see *Women's Wear Daily*, September 11, 1970, page 35.

PAGE 55 Balloon hat with beret ferrule, autumn/winter 1990. Black fur felt, unsigned. Collection Bunny Bodman
Note: For an image of this hat as shown in Cardin's autumn/winter collection, 1990–1991; see *Pierre Cardin: Past Present Future* (London and Berlin: Dirk Nishen Publishing, 1990), page 185.

PAGE 55 Black straw pillbox with pleated pink silk quill, 1980s, unsigned. Collection Bunny Bodman

PAGE 55 Sautoir of silvertone metal, long tubular beads, and lucite cylinders, late 1960s; PC monogram handtag. Collection Sandy Schreier

CHANEL

"Chanel crystals": *Women's Wear Daily*, November 25, 1927, sect. 2, page 8.
"...gold earrings studded with...": *Women's Wear Daily*, February 23, 1934, sect. 2, pages 3, 8
"...whose designs are...": *Vogue*, May 15, 1923, page 41.
"...passion for lots of...": *Women's Wear Daily*, April 8, 1931, sect. 1, page 4.
Note: "There is a group of women in Paris...": *Harper's Bazaar*, September 1, 1937, page 90.
"...when it comes to...": Bernadine Morris, *The New York Times*, March 19, 1993, B6.
"...the spirit of...": From an interview with Maxime de la Falaise McKendry in *Interview*, September 1976, page 26.

PAGE 56 2/55 bag, mid-to-late 1950s. Black quilted leather, pocket on outside, lined with deep red morocco, the interior stitched with large double C logo, otherwise unsigned, shoulder/hand strap of flat leather band run through gilt-metal chain link, with gilt-metal toggle catch. Collection Sandy Schreier
Note: The first of what is still recognized as "the Chanel bag" was introduced in 1955. According to an essay by Elisabeth Barille published in a Chanel catalogue/magazine for the spring/summer 1993 collection, the first of these was made in quilted jersey, lined with gros grain, and made by Albert Monnot. Based on its date of birth, it is known at Chanel as 2/55. The first bags were available in three sizes; four colors: beige, navy blue, brown or black and two materials, leather or jersey. It originally had a plain swivel clasp.

PAGE 57 Karl Lagerfeld for Chanel cross, Haute Couture autumn/winter 1992, probably executed by Gripoix. Rock crystal set in gilt-metal surmounted by filigree plaque set with rhinestones and faux mabé pearl, strung on a midnight navy leather cord with gilt-metal catch, unsigned. Collection Marina Schiano
Note: This cross, worn with a filmy black chiffon and lace evening dress, appears in a runway photograph featured in Melissa Richards, *Chanel Key Collections* (London: Welcome Rain Publishers, 2000), page 144. In this book the author identifies and analyzes ten pivotal collections of the house of Chanel. 1992–1993 is singled out as important because of the influences of the street. For other versions of this runway image, see *Collezioni*, Haute Couture spring/summer 1993, pages 236 and 360.

PAGE 58 Verdura style cuff, attributed to Chanel, 1930s. Faux-tortoise and gilt-metal set with pink, green, amber, blue and dark blue faceted stones, unsigned. Collection Karen Davidov
Note: With typical eclecticism (and élan), Chanel often paired the most diaphanous of lace evening gowns with clunky jeweled cuffs like this. The first such cuffs were designed for her by Verdura; his versions made with precious and semi-precious stones, along with Chanel's, have entered the firmament of fashion icons.

PAGE 59 Crystal set choker, attributed to Chanel, 1929. Crystals prong set in silvertone metal; marked: FRANCE. Private collection
Note: For illustrations of such necklaces as this, see an ad for "Chanel" reproductions made by To. Reichert & Co. in *Women's Wear Daily*, March 21, 1929, section 2, page 5.

PAGE 59 Gripoix for Chanel brooch, c. 1960. Silvertone metal set with *pâte de verre* in rose, pale blue, gray, lavender; signed plaque: CHANEL (in block letters). Collection Leslie Chin
Note: For a reprint of a 1962 Tony Palmieri photograph of Chanel wearing her brooch like this, on the hat band of her hat, see *W*, December 2001, page 62.

PAGE 60 Chanel for Aris street gloves, autumn/winter 1929. Ivory kid, the cuffs appliquéd with bands of tan and caramel; stamped: CREATION CHANEL 31, RUE CAMBON PARIS MODÈLE DÉPOSÉ AND ARIS. Collection Mark Walsh
Note: For advertisements featuring this glove, along with other elements of The Petit Ensemble (Gloves, bag, scarf, all in leather), see *Harper's Bazaar*, August 1929, page 28 and *Vogue*, September 14, 1929, page 40.

PAGE 60 Evening headdress, c. 1937. Waxed black watered silk ribbon bows mounted on black stiffened tulle base with dotted net veiling; small beige label woven in charcoal: CHANEL. Collection Mark Walsh
"Says Mademoiselle Chanel...": *Harper's Bazaar*, September 15, 1937, page 90.

PAGE 60 Jewel-set belt, autumn/winter 1932. Black calf with silvertone metal studs and bezel-set glass marble-like cabochons in rose, light green, pale blue, gray white; stamped in silver block letters: CHANEL. Collection Mark Walsh
Note: An image of this belt appeared in *Vogue*, December 1, 1932, page 32.

PAGE 61 Gripoix for Chanel necklace, c. 1938. Silvertone metal, rose, green and yolk yellow *pâte de verre*; unsigned. Collection Sandy Schreier
A drawing of a somewhat similar necklace (its petals shaped more like clover petals) described as a garland of anemone in pink crystal with red cabochons appeared in *Vogue*, March 15, 1938, page 94.

PAGE 61 Sautoir, probably made by Gripoix, c. 1930. Large pale blue crystal wheels, clear crystal beads, clear faceted discs, pale blue blown-glass beads, silvertone metal and brass fittings set with rhinestones, screw catch; unsigned. Collection Kathy Irwin

PAGE 62 Star necklace, 1939. Gilt-metal, the back of the neck a chain of stylized leaf links; signed: MADE IN FRANCE. Collection Sandy Schreier
Note: A similar necklace, with what looks like small molded flowers instead of stars was photographed by Kollar for the April 1939 *Harper's Bazaar*, page 137. See also, a version with what looks like leaf pendants *Vogue*, March 15, 1939, page 69.

PAGE 62 Pomegranate and bird necklace, 1937. Gilt-metal molded with stylized roses, pomegranates, birds and center pendant of a rose with leaves; unsigned. Collection Karen Davidov
Note: This necklace was photographed for *Harper's Bazaar*, by

Hoyningen-Huene, September 1, 1937, page 90, and also appeared in an ad for Hattie Carnegie, photographed by George Platt Lynes, *Harper's Bazaar*, October 1937, page 29. See also: *L'Officiel*, January 1938, page 82 for a sketch of the necklace, along with a matching belt.

PAGE 63—multiple pieces:

1. Sautoir, attributed to Gripoix, 1960s. Faux pearls, including tear drops set in gilt-filigree with rhinestone rondels; unsigned. Collection Mark Walsh

2. Emerald earrings, probably Robert Goosens for Chanel, c. 1960. Slightly two-tone green glass pillow-shaped stones set with rhinestones in gilt-metal molded with flowers and scrolls, baroque faux-pearl drops; stamped in block letters on small added plaque: CHANEL.
Note: Unlike mass-manufactured pieces, much of couture jewelry is hobbled together from various existent findings; thus the same findings are seen used in different sorts of ways again and again. These earrings may have originally had three drops, like the brooch that belonged to Coco Chanel, Lot 8 in the sale of the Personal Collection of Chanel, Christie's London, December 2, 1978. For a reprint of a 1962 Tony Palmieri photograph of Chanel wearing her brooch, see *W*, December 2001, page 62.

3. Faux-pearl, gilt-metal and ruby bead sautoir, 1960s; unsigned. Private collection

4. Pendant/brooch (pin removed), late 1950s. Gilt-metal with poured glass stones in green and red, unsigned. Collection Leslie Chin
Note: For a description of Chanel's own brooch like this, see the Christie's London auction catalogue of the sale of the Personal Collection of Chanel, December 2,1978, Lot 5: "This brooch was Mademoiselle Chanel's favorite piece of costume jewelry and she was often photographed wearing it—including a photograph by Willy Rizzo for *L'Express*, March 30, 1966, and another by Hatami." She wore it as well in a painting by British pop portraitist Peter Blake, 1967 (photographed for *Vogue*, December 1969, page193), and in a photograph by Richard Avedon for *Harper's Bazaar*, January 1959, page 97.

5. Robert Goossens for Chanel snake bracelet, c.1962–1969. Hinged bracelet with faceted faux- ruby eyes. Provenance: Robert Goossens archives. Private collection
Note: For an image of a bracelet with the snake head, see *Vogue*, April 15, 1969, page 77.

6. Robert Goossens for Chanel cross pendant with bezel-set stones, late 1960s. Gilt-metal with bezel-set red and green foil back poured glass stones, gilt-metal chain; stamped on plaque: CHANEL, block letters. Provenance: Robert Goossens archives. Collection Leslie Chin

7. Robert Goossens for Chanel Bar brooch/pendant, c. 1961. Baroque faux-pearls set in gilt-metal; stamped (block letters): CHANEL. Provenance: Robert Goossens archives. Collection Leslie Chin
Note: For images of the "new" Chanel bar pins, see: *Vogue*, September 1, 1961, and *Vogue*, February 1, 1962, page 155.

8. Robert Goossens for Chanel ear clips, c. 1960. Faux-pearls set in entwined circles of gilt-metal incised with floral scrolls and set with three rhinestones; unsigned. Provenance: Robert Goossens archives. Collection Leslie Chin

9. Robert Goossens for Chanel bangle bracelet, c. 1962–1969. Gilt-metal filigree with emerald glass beads. Provenance: Robert Goossens archives. Private collection

PAGE 64 Raymond Massaro for Chanel sling back shoes, c. 1960. Beige calf with black toe tips; stamped: MASSARO 2 RUE DE LA PAIX PARIS, OPERA 70-23 MODÈLE DÉPOSÉ. Collection Museum of the City of New York, 77.98.50ab, Donor: Bernice Chrysler Garbisch
Note: For a similar pair of shoes, in black and white, that originally belonged to Chanel herself, see the Christie's London auction catalogue of The Personal Collection of Chanel, December 2, 1978 Lot 102: A pair of slingback shoes of white and black by Massaro, 2 rue de la Paix. The note accompanying the lot states: "These were designed by Chanel and resembled the shoes she first designed in the 1920s and the [sic] re-launched in the 1950s."

PAGE 64 Karl Lagerfeld for Chanel cuff, spring/summer 1990. Gold painted composition set with faux baroque pearls, poured glass drops in red and green; signed: CHANEL CC © AND ® MADE IN FRANCE. Collection Christy Ferer
Note: Numerous versions of cuffs like this appeared in ads and editorial in 1990, including Chanel ads, spring 1990; *Vogue*, January 1990, page 149; and *British Vogue*, January 1990, pages 86 and 88.

PAGE 64 Gripoix for Chanel sautoir with pendant, 1983. Faux pearl necklace with gilt-metal pendant set with rose *pâte de verre* square stone, faux-pearl drop; stamped: CHANEL CC 1983. Collection Linda Hickox

PAGE 64 Karl Lagerfeld for Chanel mules, c. 1999. Black-and-white gingham cotton with black calf tips, black-and-white printed Chanel ribbon; label: CHANEL CC MADE IN ITALY. Collection Christy Ferer

PAGE 65 Karl Lagerfeld for Chanel mules, spring/summer 1992. Clear plastic with black patent tips, lucite heels, faux-pearls arranged as if in a knot; marked: CHANEL CC MADE IN ITALY. Collection Christy Ferer
Note: For an image of these mules, as worn on the street, see *The New York Times, Fashions of the Times*, fall 1992, page 66.

PAGE 65 Karl Lagerfeld for Chanel runway parure, Haute Couture, early 1990s. Probably by Gripoix, comprising: five strand dog collar of ruby faceted glass beads, gilt-metal catch; brooch/pendant of red-poured glass cabachons, ruby and amethyst faceted stones set in two shades of red composition mounted onto gilt-metal filigree plaques; ear clips of deep garnet poured glass set in gilt-metal; belt of three strands of ruby and garnet poured-glass beads with long strand ending in a poured glass drop; a ruby and a garnet glass bead five-strand bracelet with gilt-metal toggle catches; all unsigned. Collection Marina Schiano

PAGE 66 Sautoir, spring/summer 1997. Faceted faux pearls in Lucite cubes, gilt-metal CC logos, logo pearls and holograph beads; metal tag: CHANEL © AND ®, 97.CC. MADE IN FRANCE. Collection Christy Ferer

PAGE 67 Karl Lagerfeld for Chanel moon boots, autumn/winter 1996. Black quilted nylon with black patent toe tip, edged with black synthetic yak fur, wrapped in black cord run through gilt-metal chain link, the bottoms molded with treads; marked: CHANEL. Collection Sandy Schreier
For an image of these boots, in white, see *Harper's Bazaar*, August 1996, page 70.

PAGE 68 Karl Lagerfeld for Chanel cuff, 1990s. Hot pink plastic set with large foil-backed cabochons and faceted stones in red, yellow and black; signed plaque: CHANEL 2 CC 6 MADE IN FRANCE. Collection Kendra Daniel

PAGE 69 Karl Lagerfeld for Chanel logo boots and tights, Prêt-à-Porter autumn/winter 2000. Beige calf with elongated black tips, Magic Marker double C logos in black. Collection Sandy Schreier
Note: For an image of these tights and boots as worn on the runway, see *Collections Gap*, Prêt-à-Porter, autumn/winter 2000–2001, pages 11–12 and 16–18. For a photograph of Gwyneth Paltrow wearing her boots like this, with black ankle socks, see *In Style*, May 2002, page 100.

CHRISTIAN DIOR

"Over the years...": The Metropolitan Museum of Art *Bulletin*, fall 2001, page 68.

PAGE 70 Christian Dior-New York cartwheel hat, c. 1950. Black straw; labels: NAN DUSKIN and CHRISTIAN DIOR-NEW YORK INC. ® Philadelphia Museum of Art 1993.84.7, Gift of the Estate of Martha Thomas Scott

PAGE 71 Monogram brooch, oval collection, spring/summer 1951 Sterling silver set with rhinestones; French hallmarks: HG with an owl inside a diamond. Collection Leslie Chin
Note: This brooch was photographed, pinned to a fur scarf knotted around the sleeve of a grey worsted suit, by John Rawlings for *Vogue*, March 15, 1951, page 83; and reprinted in Brigid Keenan, *Dior in Vogue* (New York: Harmony Books, 1981), page 79. It was also shown attached to a black ribbon on a black and white tweed suit, photographed by Rawlings for *Vogue*, March 15, 1951, page 85; and reprinted in *Dior in Vogue*, page 80.

PAGE 72 Winged hat, c. 1950. Navy tulle small curved panel sewn with flat navy grosgrain bow and with two swoops of navy egret feathers; label: CHRISTIAN DIOR PARIS MADE IN FRANCE. Provenance: Mrs. Harvey S. Firestone Jr. Collection Sandy Schreier

PAGE 72 Leaf headdress, c. 1950. Waxed linen leaves molded with veins, sewn to green thread wrapped wires; label: CHRISTIAN DIOR PARIS MADE IN FRANCE. Collection Mark Walsh

PAGE 72 Pointed oval brooch, autumn/winter 1950. Faux-aquamarine and rhinestones set in silver-tone metal; marked: MADE IN FRANCE. Collection Leslie Chin
Note: This brooch was photographed, on the cuffed sleeve of a dark suit, by Irving Penn for *Paris Vogue*, October 1950, page 107; and reprinted in Brigid Keenan, *Dior in Vogue* (New York: Harmony Books, 1981), page 66.

PAGE 72 Roger Vivier for Christian Dior evening shoe, c. 1955. Scarlet satin with stand-up umbrella flower decoration, raised spine at toe, and intricately set rhinestone studded stiletto heel. Collection The Museum of the City of New York 79.81ab, Donor: Jennie Bell Whyte

PAGE 73 Marc Bohan for Christian Dior coiffure hat, c. 1962. Pale gray silk curls, the soft interior of organdy, lined at the front forehead with taupe tulle (for slight shaping); small label: CHRISTIAN DIOR MADE IN FRANCE. Collection: Museum of the City of New York 67.127.8. Worn by Germaine de Baume, Gift of Mr. and Mrs. Henry Rogers Benjamin
Note: Princess Grace of Monaco, a noted Dior client, wore a similar hat when she and her husband visited the White House for lunch during the Kennedy administration. For an illustration, see Betty Boyd Caroli, *America's First Ladies*, Pleasantville, New York/Montreal: The Reader's Digest Association, Inc., 1996, 85.

page 74 Chartreuse lacquered straw lampshade hat, early 1960s. Lined with taupe net, taupe grosgrain interior band; small label: CHRISTIAN DIOR MADE IN FRANCE. Collection Museum of the City of New York 67.127.3 Worn by Germaine de Baume, Gift of Mr. and Mrs. Henry Rogers Benjamin

PAGE 74 Christian Dior summer purse and cotton gloves, c. 1960. Natural straw, bone calf; gilt stamp: CHRISTIAN DIOR MADE IN FRANCE
White cotton with self embroidery; printed: SAGIL 242, RUE DE RIVOLI, PARIS. Paper tag: LES GANTS CHRISTIAN DIOR. Private collection

PAGE 75 Marc Bohan for Christian Dior day hat, early 1960s. Off-white felt topstitched in beige, label: CHRISTIAN DIOR MADE IN FRANCE. Museum of the City of New York 67.127.9. Worn by Germaine de Baume, Gift of Mr. and Mrs. Henry Rogers Benjamin

PAGE 75 Christian Dior jeweled evening pump, c. 1968. Pale beige silk crepe with ornaments of beige rhinestones, stamped: SOULIERS CHRISTIAN DIOR. Museum of City of New York 72.191.2, Donor: Mrs. Gardner Cowles (Jan)

PAGE 76 Gianfranco Ferré for Christian Dior group of rhinestone pins, early 1990s. Rhinestones set in silvertone metal, two with engine turned teal enamel; all signed with an oval plaque: CHRISTIAN DIOR BOUTIQUE. Collection Marina Schiano

PAGE 76 John Galliano for Dior Pocahontas Maasai collar, Haute Couture collection "Gare Austerlitz," autumn/winter 1998. Bone tapered tubular beads; black, red and green wooden beads; green, yellow, turquoise glass beads; textured silver tone metal chain link; tassel of horsehair, painted wooden beads and shells, Label: CHRISTIAN DIOR BOUTIQUE ®. Collection Mark Walsh
Note: For a runway image of this neckpiece, worn with a Navajo rug patterned yellow chiffon long dress, see: www.*first*VIEW.com, HC fall 1998/Christian Dior, image 53 out of 91.
For an image of a necklace similar to this, see *L'Officiel,* September 1998, page 128. See also *Paris Vogue*, September 1998, pages 95 and 113.

PAGE 76 John Galliano for Christian Dior found object belt, Haute Couture collection "La Belle et le Clochard," spring/summer 2000. Twine hung with various objects including: a crumpled paper napkin from the Paris patisserie L'Adurée, corrugated cardboard, a shard of a Wedgewood tea cup, a light green glass bead bracelet from a previous Dior collection, a champagne cork dated 2000, chandelier crystals, a tea strainer, a pocket watch, keys, safety pins, springs, straw market bag fragment, a ring from the previous Dior collection, Opera Garnier made with china craquillée and painted with a rose, edged with faux pearls; all in a soft palette featuring mint green. Collection Mark Walsh
Note: For runway images of belt/aprons like this, worn with

collage tops and a plaid pleated skirt or gray jeans-cut pants, see: *Collezioni*, spring/summer 2000, pages 181, 302 and www.*firstVIEW*.com, HC spring 2000/Christian Dior, image 36 out of 120.

PAGE 77 John Galliano for Dior wide brimmed hat, Haute Couture collection, The Wedding, autumn/winter 2000. White horsehair edged with geranium pink organza trimmed with a nosegay of lacquered silk sweet peas in fuchsia, with green stems and tendrils; label: CHRISTIAN DIOR PARIS MADE IN FRANCE. Diameter 23 inches. Collection Mark Walsh
Note: For a Michael Thompson photo of this hat, worn with a matching long dress awash with bias cut ruffles see *W*, September 2000, page 495. For a runway image, see www.*firstVIEW*.com, HC fall 2000/Christian Dior, image 12 out of 144.

JACQUES FATH

"master not of cut…": Azzedine Alaïa, telephone interview, June 1994.

PAGE 78 Hat, late 1940s. Black velvet with jutting eagle feathers in brown, black and pink/brown; label: JACQUES FATH PARIS. Collection Mark Walsh

PAGE 80 Velvet and feather hat, c. 1950. Pale blue velvet with curved shapes made from several pale blue bird's wings; label: JACQUES FATH PARIS (with scissor and Prince of Wales plume insignia.) Provenance: Mrs. Harvey S. Firestone, Jr. Collection Sandy Schreier

PAGE 81 Leaf hat, c. 1950. Emerald green fur felt with top stitching; label: JACQUES FATH PARIS. Private collection

PAGE 81 Pheasant feather-trimmed hat, c. 1948. Absinthe felt, black grosgrain hatband, black netting, yellow-dyed pheasant feathers; small white label: JACQUES FATH (with scissor and Prince of Wales plume insignia.) Collection Sandy Schreier

PAGE 81 Pump, c. 1955. Beige calf, with perforated decorations; stamped in gilt: JACQUES FATH DE PARIS, size 8 1/2 B, 51530. Private collection

JEAN PAUL GAULTIER

"…what shouldn't be shown…": *La Mode en Peinture*, spring/summer 1983, page 32.

"…surprising classicism…": *The New York Times*, September 18, 1984, B9.

PAGE 82 "Coiffe Bateau" headdress Haute Couture spring/summer 1998. Red lacquered wire strung with clear and opaque red beads, mounted on a headpiece lined with dark red velvet; unsigned. Collection Gaultier
Note: For an image of this headdress, worn with an embroidered evening gown, see: *Collezioni*, Haute Couture spring/summer 1998, page 237.

PAGE 83 Cuff, autumn/winter 1986, Russe collection. Silvertone metal inscribed with the date: LXXXVI; unsigned. Collection Karen Davidov

PAGE 84 High-heeled sneakers, c. 1989. Navy canvas, white rubber, hand painted orange stripe; Star logo Junior Gaultier and label: JUNIOR GAULTIER. Collection Titi Halle

PAGE 84 Christian Louboutin for Jean Paul Gaultier toe shoe flats, 1998. Chocolate brown leather; label: GAULTIER PARIS PAR CHRISTIAN LOUBOUTIN. Private collection
Note: Christian Louboutin made a whole collection of toe shoes, from sporty flats to bejeweled evening sandals. For example, see: *Paris Vogue*, September 1988, pages 216, 225, and 254; *L'Officiel*, March 1998, page 136 and August 1998, page 159.

PAGE 85 Fan headdress, Haute Couture, autumn/winter 2001. Black hair wrapped sticks with coiled black rope at bottom, dangling shanks of synthetic hair; unsigned. Collection Gaultier
Note: For an image of this headdress as worn on the runway, see *L'Officiel 1000 Modèles*, Haute Couture - Paris- winter, August-September, 2001, page 16.

PAGE 85 Fringed purse, Haute Couture autumn/winter 2001. Metallic red patent leather with black metal catch, black patent leather leaves and bugs, and long black bugle-beaded fringes; label: (in black net and lace) Gaultier Paris. Collection Gaultier.
Note: For an image of this purse as shown on the runway, see *L'Officiel 1000 Modèles* Haute Couture - Paris- winter August–September, 2001, page 17.

PAGE 85 Chinese bib necklace, Haute Couture autumn/winter 2001. Red painted metal set with red rhinestones with tremblant dragonflies and butterflies; unsigned. Collection Gaultier
Note: For an image of this necklace as worn on the runway, see *L'Officiel 1000 Modèles* Haute Couture - Paris- winter August–September, 2001, page 14.

ROMEO GIGLI

PAGE 86 Romeo Gigli dangling earrings, spring/summer 1990. Venetian glass in clear, red and gold; unsigned. Collection Holly Brubach
Note: For images of earrings from this collection, see: *British Vogue*, January 1990, page 69 and March 1990, page 269.

PAGE 86 Romeo Gigli chandelier earrings, autumn/winter 1989. Micro-mosaic floral medallions set in brass tone metal; unsigned. Collection Holly Brubach.
Note: A photograph of Romeo Gigli's wife, Sara, wearing earrings similar to these, appeared in *Harpers & Queen*, August 2001, page 62.

PAGE 86 Romeo Gigli knot shoes, 1989. Iridescent deep peridot taffeta with shaped court heels; stamped: ROMEO GIGLI MADE IN ITALY. Collection Sandy Schreier
Note: For a red version of this shoe, see *Taxi*, August 1989.

PAGE 87 Belt, c. 1990. Brown leather with grommet decorations, darkened metal buckle; stamped: ROMEO GIGLI. Collection Holly Brubach

GIVENCHY

"…pure…all line.": *Vogue*, April 15, 1963, page 66, 70.
"Givenchy blows air…": *Harper's Bazaar*, May 1960.
"With his fall-winter 1959…": Hamish Bowles, *Jacqueline Kennedy: The White House Years*, New York: The Metropolitan Museum of Art; Boston, New York, London: A Bulfinch Press Book/Little Brown and Company, 2001.

PAGE 88 Wave hat, Haute Couture, autumn/winter 1988. Candy pink satin over buckram mounted on a black velvet pillbox; handwritten label: 36 JOSÉE. Collection Philadephia Museum of Art, 1993-52-3, purchased with funds contributed by an anonymous donor

Note: The autumn/winter 1988 Givenchy collection emphasized bright colors.

PAGE 90 White cotton hat, spring/summer 1968. Arced panels jutting out from a small skull cap of straw overlaid with cotton. Philadelphia Museum of Art, 1993.52.1, purchased with funds contributed by an anonymous donor
Note: For a photograph of a hat like this, being fitted on the head of a model by head milliner Halston of Bergdorf Goodman, see Walter Vecchio, *The Fashion Makers A Photographic Record*, text by Robert Riley, New York: Crown Publishers, Inc., 1968, 111. The custom millinery salon of Bergdorf Goodman was known for its original Paris models of couture hats.

PAGE 90 Bowler hat, c. 1963. Midnight navy straw with wreath of folded straw; label: GIVENCHY PARIS MADE IN FRANCE. Collection Philadelphia Museum of Art, 1993.52.2, purchased with funds contributed by an anonymous donor

PAGE 90 Evening bag, c. 1965. Cocoa silk gazar with rhinestone-pavé oval ring handle; stamped in gilt- block letters: GIVENCHY. Collection The Bruce Museum, Greenwich, Connecticut, Gift of Joan Simpson Raines

PAGE 91 Boa, c. 1980. Royal blue and creamy white china silk, and tulle; label: GIVENCHY PARIS. Collection Mark Walsh

HALSTON

"Making hats is…": *Esquire*, August, 1975, page 138.

PAGE 91 Toque, c. 1966. Pony stenciled in black; label: BY HALSTON OF BERGDORF GOODMAN. Collection Philadelphia Museum of Art 1993.93.2, Gift of Kay Hunt

PAGE 93 Elsa Peretti for Halston wrist cuff, c. 1971. Carved ivory, unsigned. Collection Museum of the City of New York 86.154.22, donor Ms. Lauren Bacall
Note: A cuff like this was photographed for *Vogue*, November 15, 1971, page 105 (in silver) and page 106 (in ivory).

PAGE 94 Elsa Peretti for Tiffany & Co. belt, first designed 1969. Black leather, sterling silver; stamped: ELSA PERETTI STERLING TIFFANY & CO. - STERLING. Collection Adeline Tintner Janowitz
Note: A belt like this, designed by Elsa Peretti for Halston, was photographed for *Vogue*, October

1971, page 105. It was shown with a typically casual 1970s ensemble of sleeveless yellow ribbed turtle neck, narrow and long, worn with pencil thin black leggings. Elsa Peretti went to work for Tiffany & Co. in 1974, so this example can be dated as 1974 or later. For a photograph of Liza Minelli wearing her belt like this, performing in denim pants, white turtleneck and red cardigan tied around her shoulders, see: *Vogue*, February 1974. See also: *Vogue*, November 15, 1971, page 105 and the cover of *British Vogue*, December 1989.

PAGE 95 Disco sandal, c. 1981. Metallic red leather edged with silver piping, the self bow centered with a small red enameled gilt-metal flower, stamped: HALSTON MADE IN ITALY. Collection Sandy Schreier
Note: For Andy Warhol polaroids of a selection of shoes by Halston, including this one see: *Halston*, Steven Bluttal, editor. (New York: Phaidon Press, Inc., 2001) pages 468–469.

CHARLES JAMES

"…an exuberant sculpture…": *Flair*, May 1950 page 46.

PAGE 96 Black velvet "Nanny's" cap with tapered black satin ribbon streamers, 1948; label of white satin ribbon handwritten in blue: CHARLES JAMES 48. Collection Sandy Schreier

PAGE 97 Lappet scarf, late 1940s-early 1950s. Navy faille taffeta and deep peridot silk satin; unsigned. Collection Sandy Schreier
"Arcs in reverse…": Elizabeth Ann Coleman, *The Genius of Charles James*, New York: The Brooklyn Museum and Holt, Rinehart and Winston, 1982, page 85.

PAGE 97 Candlestand evening bag, early 1950s. Light gray/blue silk satin, cut in the shape of a soft mug with self tie to gather in the top; unsigned. Provenance: Muriel Bultman Francis. Collection Sandy Schreier

LACROIX

"For Lacroix a Triumph…": *The New York Times*, July 27, 1987.

PAGE 98 Boot sandals, Prêt-à-Porter, spring/summer 1994. Natural straw, chocolate calf and gilt-metal studs; hot pink satin label: CHRISTIAN LACROIX PARIS, stamped: MADE IN ITALY. Private collection

PAGE 99 Large cross pendant, Haute Couture, autumn/winter

1989–1990. Gilt-metal set with black or brick red cabochons; marked: CHRISTIAN LACROIX MADE IN FRANCE. Collection Christian Lacroix

PAGE 100 Sunglasses, Haute Couture, spring/summer 1991. Tinted lenses in gilt-wire frames applied with bright orange branch coral studded with rhinestones; marked: CL CHRISTIAN LACROIX Collection Christian Lacroix
Note: For an image of a model wearing a brilliant yellow short ball gown, holding these glasses, see *Vogue*, April 1991, page 288.

PAGE 100 Christian Lacroix for Monet cross pendant/brooch, spring/summer 1992 gilt-metal, signed: CHRISTIAN LACROIX BIJOUX. Collection Margery Rubin
Note: A brooch like this belonged to Jacqueline Kennedy Onassis and was included in the Sotheby's April 23–26, 1996, auction of property from her estate. A photograph of her wearing it on December 3, 1993, accompanies Lot 540 in the catalogue.

PAGE 100 Heart with cross brooch, 1989. Gilt-metal set with pink and purple rhinestones; signed: NOEL 89 and CL PARIS CHRISTIAN LACROIX. Collection Christy Ferer
Note: A photograph of a pin like this appears in the book: Francois Baudot, *Christian Lacroix* Paris: Universe/Vendome, 1997, page 18.

PAGE 100 Heart brooch, 1994. Darkened gilt-metal cast with scrolls and set with chips of mother-of-pearl as well as with a small black and white cameo; signed: CL CHRISTIAN LACROIX MADE IN FRANCE. Collection Christy Ferer

PAGE 100 Heart brooch, 1992. Gilt-metal set with pale pink, amethyst, ruby and topaz rhinestones; signed: CL WITH A STAR, NOEL 1992. Collection Christy Ferer

PAGE 100 Floral spray brooch, spring/summer 1994. Gilt-metal set with bright almost flourescent glass surmounted with black glass highlights; signed: CHRISTIAN LACROIX E94 MADE IN FRANCE. Courtesy Doyle New York

PAGE 100 Triple flower pin, Haute Couture, spring/summer 1996 Gilt-metal set with rhinestones in shades of purple, fuchsia, pink, green and pale yellow; signed: CHRISTIAN LACROIX CL MADE IN FRANCE. Courtesy Doyle New York

PAGE 101   Pirate hat, Luxe collection, spring/summer 1988. Natural straw with bows of black grosgrain; unsigned. Collection Lars Nillson
Note: For an image of this hat, in velvet, see *W*, August 24–31, 1987, and *Joyce*, September/October 1987, page 255.

PAGE 102   Evening bag, Haute Couture, autumn/winter 1990. Gold/olive satin overlaid on one side with gilt-metal set with faceted stones in orange, citrine, red, and on the other with a hammered gilt-metal plaque; marked: CL. Collection Christian Lacroix
Note: For a photograph of a pochette like this, see *Paris Vogue*, September 1990, page 228.

PAGE 102   Evening bag, Haute Couture, autumn/winter 2000. Quilted turquoise green silk satin, the reverse and the flap densely embroidered with a tapestry of chenille, braid, bugle beads, shaped sequins, rhinestones and dangling rhinestone bands; marked: CHRISTIAN LACROIX.
Collection Christian Lacroix

PAGE 103   Dog collar, Haute Couture, autumn/winter 1997. Chain link and various stones including slices of tinted agate with Victorian style metal asps set with faux pearls and rhinestones, turquoise chips, lapis chips, fool's gold (pyrite) and foil-backed beads; tag: CHRISTIAN LACROIX CL MADE IN FRANCE. Collection Christian Lacroix

PAGE 103   Jeweled armadillo bag, Haute Couture, spring/summer 2001. Gilt-metal set with rhinestones with spine of gilt-metal chain link. the other side of blue/green glitter overlaid with a plaid design of blue tinted metal wire, chain link and turquoise chains; gilt-metal tag: CL CHRISTIAN LACROIX MADE IN FRANCE. Collection Christian Lacroix
Note: For a runway image of a model carrying this piece, see *Collezioni*, Haute Couture Spring/Summer 2001, page 232. Her almost-but-not-quite conservative ensemble consists of a black coat with fringe, a tomato red blouse with stock tie, and white pleated just below the knee length skirt sewn with stripes of square sequins.

PAGE 104   Black velvet stiletto heel shoes, Haute Couture, autumn/winter 2001. Copper leather appliqué, two tone copper/bronze metal heel; marked: CHRISTIAN LACROIX PARIS.

Collection Christian Lacroix.
Note: These shoes were used extensively in the couture winter 2001–2002 collection, and shown with evening dresses of every length as well as with flared lace trousers worn under dresses.

PAGE 104   Silver glitter nail gloves, Haute Couture, autumn/winter 2001. Black stretch satin hand painted with silver glitter nails and scrolling foliage; label: CHRISTIAN LACROIX PARIS. Collection Christian Lacroix

PAGE 105   Ankle boots, Prêt-à-Porter, autumn/winter 1997. Brown satin with gold plastic cutaway wedges; stamped: BAZAAR DE CHRISTIAN LACROIX. Private collection
Note: For images of these boots, as worn on the runway, see *Collections Gap*, Autumn/Winter 1997–1998, page 122–3

KARL LAGERFELD

"For Chloë's '78 collection...": *Vogue*, August 1979 page 222.

PAGE 106   Kirsten Woodward for Karl Lagerfeld slipper chair hat, autumn/winter 1985. Bright red synthetic satin with yellow tassels. Collection Karen Davidov
Note: A hat like this was photographed for *Vanity Fair*, September 1985, page 98, worn with a little black dress with wide spreading collar.

PAGE 107   Ugo Correani for Karl Lagerfeld biscuit necklace, autumn/winter 1984. Pink painted composition set with rhinestones, pink cord; metal plaque: U. CORREANI MADE IN ITALY. Collection Louise Doktor

PAGE 108   Belt, spring/summer 1986. Gold leather; signed: KARL LAGERFELD. Collection Joan Phillips
Note: Several images of this belt appeared in *Paris Vogue*, February 1986, pages 113, 115 and 146, as well as in numerous issues of *W*, in October and November 1985.

PAGE 108   Ugo Correani for Karl Lagerfeld for Chloë guitar brooch, spring/summer 1983. Blue and orange composition set with mirror, rhinestones, fishing line; Paper label: UGO CORREANI, metal plaque: U. CORREANI MADE IN ITALY. Collection Louise Doktor

PAGE 108   Ugo Correani for Karl Lagerfeld for Chloë Joseph Hoffman-inspired brooch, autumn/winter 1984
Gold painted metal set with mottled glass cabochons. Signed: Ugo

Correani for Karl Lagerfeld. Collection Louise Doktor

PAGE 109   Ugo Correani for Karl Lagerfeld choker, autumn/winter 1983. Silvertone metal shower head dripping rhinestones and faux pearls, unsigned. Collection Museum of the City of New York 89.92.8a, Donor: Fashion Design Department, Parsons School of Design

PAGE 109   Ugo Correani for Karl Lagerfeld. Hot and cold earrings, autumn/winter 1983. Silvertone metal faucet heads set with cornflower blue or pink rhinestones, unsigned. Museum of the City of New York 89.92.7ab Donor: Fashion Design Department, Parsons School of Design
Note: For an image of earrings like these, worn with a long white dress, its bodice like a double-breasted blazer tucked into a jeans style skirt, see Chloë advertisement, *Vogue*, September 1983, page 401.

PAGE 109   Ugo Correani for Karl Lagerfeld pastry necklace, autumn/winter 1984. Composition and string; metal tag: U. CORREANI MADE IN ITALY, paper tag: UGO CORREANI, HAND WRITTEN X KARL LAGERFELD. Courtesy Doyle New York

PAGE 109   Vegetable necklace, late 1980s. Matte gilt-metal, faux pearls, plastic in deep colors, signed: KARL LAGERFELD. Courtesy Doyle New York

PAGE 110   Ugo Correani for Karl Lagerfeld for Chloë spool necklace, spring/summer 1984. Green, black and gold painted composition set with rhinestones; unsigned. Collection Louise Doktor

PAGE 111   Ugo Correani for Karl Lagerfeld for Chloë pincushion brooch and earrings, spring/summer 1984. Silver and/or gold painted metal, composition; rhinestones and pearl or bead top pins, the brooch signed with paper tag: UGO CORREANI; earrings unsigned. Collection Louise Doktor

PAGE 111   Ugo Correani for Karl Lagerfeld for Chloë needle and thread brooch, spring/summer 1984. Silvertone metal set with rhinestones; unsigned. Collection Louise Doktor
Note: A brooch like this, worn with an oversize flannel pea jacket over long pleated skirt was photographed for *Town & Country*, February 1984, page 117.

JEANNE LANVIN

"...the most important...": *Vogue*, November 15, 1927, page 160.

"Her famous blue...": ibid.

PAGE 112   Turban, c. 1910. Ivory satin with black straw crown and black stripped feathers; label: JEANNE LANVIN 16 RUE BOISSY-D'ANGLAIS PARIS. Private collection

PAGE 112   Embroidered reticule, c. 1922–1924. Pale greenish yellow sheer silk over China silk embroidered with silver metal chain stitch, small slightly opalescent glass beads and clear bugle beads; label: JEANNE LANVIN 22 FAUBOURG ST. HONORÉ PARIS. Collection Mark Walsh

PAGE 114   Wide brimmed hat, c. 1910. Deep purple velvet with a brown mink hatband, the upturned brim trimmed with silk velvet fern fronds, pale lilac-pink lilacs, roses and other flowers; label: JEANNE LANVIN 22, FAUBOURG ST. HONORÉ PARIS. Collection Sandy Schreier

PAGE 114   Hat, c. 1920. Navy silk taffeta, padded flowers cut from patterned velvet flowers, brocade flowers and pressed velvet leaves, all with wide silk piping, label: Jeanne Lanvin 22, Faubourg St. Honoré Paris. Philadelphia Museum of Art, Gift of Margaret S. Hinchman 1951.21.14

PAGE 115   Machine Age purse, c. 1925. Aluminum enameled in black, with braided metallic thread handle; the catch impressed: LANVIN FRANCE; the interior stamped in gilt: LANVIN FRANCE. Collection Christy Mayer Lefkowith

PAGE 115   Hat and muff, early 1930s. Cerise velvet arranged in coils; label: JEANNE LANVIN PARIS 3411 22 FAUBOURG ST. HONORÉ . Collection Mark Walsh

CLAIRE MCCARDELL

"Until recently only...": *Life*, August 23, 1954, page 77.

PAGE 116   Gloves, c. 1954. Gingham check cotton, white cotton palms, white cotton knit edging; unsigned, original plastic wrapper printed with graph paper check printed: CLAIRE MCCARDELL. Private collection

PAGE 116   Sunglasses, summer 1955 Red, white and black plastic, green lenses; marked: CLAIRE MCCARDELL. Private collection
Note: For an ad featuring these and other Claire McCardell "sunspecs," see *Vogue*, April 1955, page 42.

PAGE 116   Belt, late 1940s. Red elastic with fastening of twisted gilt metal hooks and eyes, brass studs unsigned. Collection Mark Walsh

ISSEY MIYAKE

"Clearly Miyake has...": *Newsweek*, October 7, 1983, page 85.

PAGE 119   Drawstring purse, spring/summer 1995. Hot pink synthetic taffeta crinkled and arranged in jester points, lavender cord with silvertone metal tips, unsigned. Collection Nancy S. Knox

PAGE 120   Naoki Takizawa for Issey Miyake Flat purse/Box purse, autumn/winter 2001. Brown leather. Collection Nancy S. Knox

PAGE 121   Drawstring purse, autumn/winter 1994. Black synthetic taffeta lined with golden yellow; label ISSEY MIYAKE. Collection Nancy S. Knox

PAGE 121   Sahara spectacles, first shown spring/summer 1983. Wood; unlabeled. Collection Issey Miyake
Note: For images of spectacles like these see *La Mode en Peinture*, March/April/May 1984, page 71; *Harper's Bazaar*, March 1984, page 314; and Caroline Rennolds Milbank, *Couture The Great Designers*, New York: Stewart, Tabori, and Chang, 1985, page 114.

PAGE 121   Dreadlocks hat, autumn/winter 1985. Greige and blue wool; label: ISSEY MIYAKE, second label: SAMPLE NO. EP070005 WOOL 100% M. D. S. MADE IN JAPAN. Collection Issey Miyake

MOSCHINO

"Unlike such iconoclastic...". Ben Brantley, "Designing Anarchist" *Vanity Fair*, March 1990, page 78.

PAGE 122   Flat shoes, spring/summer 1992. Black or pale bone suede machine embroidered with black or ivory with the outcry: FASHION/FASHOFF, stamped: MOSCHINO. Collection Sandy Schreier

PAGE 123   Double-yolk Latex brooch, spring/summer 1988. Latex with brass pins; unsigned. Collection Moschino

PAGE 124   Collection of Moschino jewels, spring/summer 1996

1. Heart bib necklace, spring/summer 1996. Red patent leather hearts connected by blackened metal links; unsigned. Collection Karen Davidov

2. Love letter sautoir, spring/summer 1996. White felt envelopes sealed with red felt kisses, red crystal beads and red felt rosebuds; Paper tag: MOSCHINO BIJOUX 75 PRODOTTO E DISTRIBUITO DA: SISSI ROSSI S. L. R - VIA MANIN 1/M 40129 BOLOGNA ART.29 - MADE IN ITALY. Collection Karen Davidov

3. Heart pendant necklace, spring/summer 1996. Faux pearls Interspersed with red hot candy beads, the pendant with heart prayer votive set inside clear glass; unsigned. Collection Karen Davidov

4. Peace symbol necklace, spring/summer 1996. Pale aqua sandwich glass stones, clear glass tear drops, wrapped gilt metal wire and black velvet ribbon bows; paper tag: MOSCHINO BIJOUX 141 PRODOTTO E DISTRIBUITO DA: SISSI ROSSI S. L. R VIA MANIN 1/M 40129 BOLOGNA ART. 42 MADE IN ITALY. Collection Karen Davidov

5. Mirror, Mirror necklace, spring/summer 1996. Black velvet ribbon choker with hand mirror pendant, the mirror printed on one side with: "Mirror, mirror on the wall, Who is the fairest of them all?" And on the other side with: "Specchio Specchio della mie brame, Chi é la piu bella del Reame?" Collection Karen Davidov

6. Cat necklace, spring/summer 1996. Black cat pendant composed of tubular and cat head beads, clear fish beads; and opaque white milk bottle beads, metal plaque: MOSCHINO. Collection Karen Davidov

7. Toy necklace, spring/summer 1996. Black and red beads, pendant of articulated doll with fruit basket hat; metal plaque: MOSCHINO. Collection Karen Davidov

8. Long bon-bon necklace, spring/summer 1996. Clear beads with composition sweets, some decorated with embroidered floral appliqués, the pendant a pink after-dinner mint suspending a heart shaped leaf with ladybug; metal tag: MOSCHINO. Collection Karen Davidov

9. Dangling earrings, spring/summer 1996; Heart-shaped composition leaf with ladybug suspending a pea pod; metal tag: MOSCHINO. Collection Karen Davidov
Note: A runway photo of a model wearing earrings like these appears in the spring/summer season 1996

Moschino catalogue titled: *Plus ça change, plus c'ést la même chose.*

PAGE 125 Napoleonic coat-hanger headdress, autumn/winter 1988. Fur coat hanger mounted on a taffeta-covered headband, the hanger labeled: MOSCHINO FUR FOR FUN, with signature red heart. Collection Moschino
Note: For an image of this headdress as shown in a runway tableau, see *X Anni di Kaos!* 1983–1993 Franco Moschino and Lida Castelli, editors. Milan: Edizioni Lybra Immagine 1993. See also *British Vogue*, September 1988, page 303.

PAGE 125 Airplane hat, spring/summer 1988. Model G.I. Joe toy plane mounted on black straw pillbox; hand written label: MOSCHINO. Collection Moschino
Note: For images of this hat, see *Harpers & Queen*, July 1988, page 245, and Moschino ads in *Paris Vogue*, February 1988, page 37; March 1988, page 204; and *British Vogue*, March 1988, page 51.

PAGE 125 Millenium pocketbook, 2000. Lilac cotton velvet wrapped with iridescent sheer lilac/green ribbon, the brick red silk flower with velvet leaves, bone leather tag printed in black: "HAPPY 2000!" Private collection
Note: For a runway image of a model carrying this pocketbook, see www.*first*VIEW.com, 1999, Moschino, image 10 of 24.

PAGE 125 Cloud Kelly bag, spring/summer 1990. Pale blue suede with ivory suede cloud appliqué, gilt-metal tag "Centopercento Moschino Red Wall ®, 443754, Made in Italy. Collection Moschino
Note: For an image of a smaller version of this bag, see *The New York Times*, February 25, 1990, page 52, with the caption: "cloudy 'baby Kelly' bag by Franco Moschino, $630 at Saks Fifth Avenue."

POIRET

"name remains indissolubly...": Yvonne Deslandres, *Poiret*, New York: Rizzoli, 1987, 220.

PAGE 126 Directoire inspired wide brimmed hat, c. 1909. Cream crepe over buckram frame, silk flowers; label: PAUL POIRET À PARIS and FLORETTE, 453 FIFTH AVENUE. Collection Wadsworth Atheneum, Gift of the heirs of Dorothea Thompson, 1967.78

PAGE 127 Attributed to Raoul Dufy for Martine parasol, spring/summer 1914. Silk charmeuse shade and pouf printed with black outlined flowers and leaves in shades of green, rose, sky blue and ivory, the handle with carved in one knob and elongated ferrule of dark wood; button incised: B. ALTMAN & CO. * N.Y.* Collection Sandy Schreier.
Note: For an example of a Poiret/Martine/B. Altman parasol, in the same shape as this but in a different pattern, see *Harper's Bazaar*, July 1914, page 54. The caption justifies the elongated handle: "so it may top the tallest hat."

PAGE 128 Turban, attributed to Poiret, c. 1910. Bright red Liberty silk designed as a soft split drape to be wrapped around the head and fastened with a flat self button embroidered with stylized flower in beads of blue, red, green, yellow, blue and black; unsigned. Collection Mark Walsh
Note: "An editorial in *The Queen* in 1910 describing a Poiret collection shows that he was obtaining some of his fabrics from Liberty—and possibly some of his ideas as well: 'This season there is evidently a general leaning towards the Oriental, which expresses itself definitely in turbans and Indian cashmeres. Every mannequin had her pretty head enveloped in a coloured silk handkerchief, twisted like a turban, and in a shade to go with her gown.'" Alison Adburgham, *Liberty's: A Biography of a Shop*. London: George Allen & Unwin Ltd., 1975, page 90.

PAGE 129 Pansy trimmed hat, early 1910s. Lacquered natural straw with crown of purple China silk sewn overall with velvet pansies in shades of amber, orange and purple, trimmed with a wide bow of ribbon printed with narrow black and white stripes and small sprays of roses, the inside brim lined with further black and white striped, floral printed ribbon; label: PAUL POIRET À PARIS. Collection Mark Walsh

PAGE 129 Perugia for Poiret evening shoes, c. 1924. Pearl gray plush (with a pinkish cast) with "Persian leaf" appliqués in silver kid, the curved heels studded with rhinestones in shades of blue, emerald, lavender, rose, lime and topaz; stamped: PERUGIA BTÉ S. G. D. G. 21 AVENUE N. DAMES - NICE 11. FAUBG ST - HONORÉ PARIS; oval sticker: MODÈLE DÉPOSÉ PRE 3806 NO/2919. Museum of the City of NewYork 40.153.2ab, Donor: Mrs. George Blumenthal
Note: For similarly decorated Perugia shoes, see a pair of T-strap sandals described in *Vogue*, December 1, 1956, as being by Perugia for Poiret, c. 1918; see also a pair of maroon velvet and gold kid T-strap sandals, *Vogue*, December 15, 1924, page 56, listed as Perugia, with no mention of Poiret. For a pump with similar appliqué, part of the Colin Poiret collection and described in the caption as "A Perugia creation for Paul Poiret," see: *Paul Poiret* By Yvonne Deslandres, Rizzoli, New York, 1987, page 226.

PAGE 130 Rosine Advertising fan, c. 1920. Balsa sticks and paper leaf printed with Georges Lepape image of an odalisque clad in typical Poiret orientalist finery, the reverse printed with the name of perfumes offered by Rosine, Poiret's perfume company. Collection Sandy Schreier

PAGE 131 Madeleine Panizon for Poiret hat, c. 1923. Tomato kid leather, cut-out and sewn with gilt-braid lines and circles, over black silk satin with gold mesh. Philadelphia Museum of Art, Gift of Vera White 1951.126.3b

YVES SAINT LAURENT

"Most talked about...": *Vogue*, March 1, 1962, page 126.
"You can compare...": *Women's Wear Daily*, July 26, 1968, page 4.
"There is no...": *Women's Wear Daily*, September 17, 1968, front page.
"Nothing gave a...": *The New York Times*, October 14, 2000 Section B, page 8.

PAGE 132 Necklace, 1987. Resin in pale shades of amber, smoky topaz, mint green and pale mottled blue-green set in gilt-metal; signed on rectangular tag: YSL. Private collection
Note: This bib necklace was widely photographed at the time. See *Vogue*, June 1987, page 215, for a Guy Bourdin photograph of a model wearing it with a short evening dress with a long, covered-up black bodice and flippy short blue pouf skirt.

PAGE 133 Peace dove earrings, c. 1988. Gilt-metal; marked: YSL. Collection Kendra Daniel

PAGE 134 Roger Scemana for Yves Saint Laurent heart talisman necklace, spring/summer, 1962. Blackened silvertone metal set with faux rubies, diamonds, and pearls. Collection Yves Saint Laurent
Note: For a photograph of the first appearance of this necklace, see *Le Supplement aux Collections de la haute couture de Paris*, spring/summer 1962. For an undated photograph of Yves Saint Laurent in his white smock, clutching the heart to his own heart, see *Yves Saint Laurent par Yves Saint Laurent*, Paris: Editions Herscher, 1986, 205.

PAGE 134 Black-and-white pearl earrings, first shown spring/summer 1962. Baroque faux button pearls set in squares of blackened metal pavé with black rhinestones; unsigned. Collection Margery Rubin
Note: Earrings like this appeared so often with Yves Saint Laurent clothes as to be practically ubiquitous. For several examples, see *Paris Vogue*, March 1962, pages 201,203,233, and 237; *Vogue*, March 1, 1962, page 125, September 1, 1962, pages 163–164 and *Harper's Bazaar*, November 1965, cover. In 1962, *Paris Vogue* credited Roger Jean-Pierre with their design. In 1963 *Vogue* credit for earrings like this was given to Roger Scemana.

PAGE 135 Fur trimmed hat, Haute Couture, autumn/winter 1962. Deep charcoal velvet trimmed with ivory mink; small label: YVES SAINT LAURENT. Collection Museum of the City of New York 82.42.15, Gift of Mrs. Andrew Strong White

PAGE 135 Yves Saint Laurent leather hat, Haute Couture, autumn/winter 1966. Black leather with gilt-metal pyramid studs, edged with black sheared beaver; small label: YVES SAINT LAURENT. Collection Museum of the City of New York 82.42.34, Gift of Mrs. Andrew Strong White
Note: Versions of this hat appeared in *Harper's Bazaar*, September 1966, page 271, photographed by Hiro. The two models were wearing gold nailhead studded ensembles as well, one in brown jersey, one in black leather.

PAGE 136 Hat, Imperial China collection, autumn/winter 1977. Black velvet edged with black braid with tassels of black and royal blue; small label: YVES SAINT LAURENT PARIS. Museum of the City of New York 82.42.41, Donor: Mrs. Andrew Strong White

PAGE 137 Bib necklace, spring/summer 1991. Gilt-metal set with an assortment of stones including tortoise sanded glass drops, trade beads and mottled red glass square faceted stones; gilt metal tag: YVES SAINT LAURENT RIVE GAUCHE MADE IN FRANCE. Collection Kendra Daniel
Note: A necklace like this, in shades of blue, worn with a bright pink Zouave jacket, appeared in spring 1991 Rive Gauche ads.

PAGE 138 Roger Vivier for Yves Saint Laurent pumps with Pilgrim buckles, c. 1965. Bright gold kid, gilt-metal buckles; stamped: ROGER VIVIER PARIS. Museum of the City of New York, 77.98.45 Gift of Bernice Chrysler Garbisch

PAGE 138 Drawstring purse, Haute Couture, autumn/winter 1988. Purple suede sewn with gilt-metal bow tied bunch of grapes; the three dimensional metal bow above a stitched down stem of bronze cord, the grapes of various sized gilt metal studs; black cord handles with purple suede tassels; purple suede label: YVES SAINT LAURENT. Private Collection

PAGE 138 Chain belt, first shown 1967. Tortoise plastic discs and darkened metal; unsigned. Collection Joan Phillips

PAGE 139 Passementerie pocketbook, c. 1997. Olive cord with faux tortoise handles; label: YVES SAINT LAURENT - MADE IN FRANCE. Private collection

PAGE 139 Envelope with shaped flap, late 1990s. Pale butterscotch straw; label: YVES SAINT LAURENT. Private collection

PAGE 139 Passementerie shoulder bag, summer 2001. Chocolate cord with braid and ball strap; no label. Private collection

PAGE 140 Belt, 1980s. Sapphire and emerald braid sewn with loops of fluted gilt-metal beads interspersed with floss covered beads, rounded button knobs hand embroidered with a bead-studded lattice; hammered metal tag in the shape of a heart incised: YVES SAINT LAURENT RIVE GAUCHE PARIS. Collection Christy Ferer
Note: "At Yves Saint Laurent..." *Women's Wear Daily*, January 26, 1968, page 10.

PAGE 140 Art Nouveau revival necklace, 1970s. Ceramic poppies in royal blue, red speckled with darker red strung with large nacre beads, black and turquoise beads, faux pearls, one pendant tassel of faux tear drops on chain link, another of hat pin pearl drops; unsigned. Collection Sandy Schreier

PAGE 141 Ebony collar, c. 1983. Elongated wood beads interspersed with silvertone metal elements set with rhinestones; unsigned. Collection Kendra Daniel

PAGE 141 Art Deco revival necklace, c. 1983. Black plastic and rhinestones; unsigned. Collection Sandy Schreier
Note: A necklace like this, shown with a glittery leopard print plunging neckline dress, appeared in an ad in *Vogue Italia*, September 1983, (unpaginated); similar bracelets were shown in *Harper's Bazaar*, October 1983, page 221.

PAGE 142 Rive Gauche rock crystal choker, autumn/winter 1988. Gilt-metal wire; metal tag: YSL and MADE IN FRANCE. Collection Sandy Schreier
Note: A choker like this was photographed for *Elle*, November 1988, pages 249 and 251.

PAGE 142 Tassel necklace, 1980s. *Pâte de verre* lozenge beads in shades of mottled purple, brown and rose strung on black passementerie cord with tassel; unsigned. Collection Leslie Chin

PAGE 142 Necklace, 1990s. Large nugget beads in purply blue, green, lobster-red, and white/tan with orange maltese cross; unsigned. Private collection

PAGE 142 Sautoir, 1970s. Polished peach pits strung on knotted string; unsigned. Collection Joan Phillips

PAGE 142 Tribal mask drop earrings, c. 1991. Ceramic glazed in green and copper, tear-drop stones in brown and olive backed with textured silver fabric, tear drop faux emeralds, hollow brass beads; unsigned. Collection Kendra Daniel

PAGE 142 Necklace, Haute Couture, spring/summer 1988. Faux pearl necklace and *pâte de verre*; unsigned. Collection Sandy Schreier
Note: For an Arthur Elgort photograph of a model wearing this necklace with a floor length black satin evening suit with white notched lapel collar, see *Mode 1958–1990 Yves Saint Laurent*, Sezon Museum of Art, 1990, 95; a similar piece appeared in *W*, August 1988, pages 8–15.

PAGE 144 Boots, Imperial China collection, Prêt-à-Porter, autumn/winter 1977. Black suede with tall straight gold kid heels trimmed with flat black and gold braid and with black and gold

twisted cords, marked: FAIT MAIN and YVES SAINT LAURENT. Collection Marina Schiano
Note: For an image of boots like this, see *Paris Vogue,* September 1977, page 332, and November 1977, page 108. The Imperial China collection featured many variations of ensembles with long, flowing skirts (day and evening) or pants gathered in at the ankle, Cossack/mandarin jackets with full sleeves, tasseled cord belts, scarves and shawls, and fur-edged hats.

PAGE 145 Gauntlets, Imperial China collection, Haute Couture, autumn/winter 1977. Gold leather trimmed with brown mink with drawstring cuffs and tasseled drawstrings; unsigned. Collection Marina Schiano
Note: Photographs of gloves like these appear in *Yves Saint Laurent Images of Design 1958–1988*, New York: Alfred A. Knopf, 1988, pages 116 and 119, as well as in *Paris Vogue*, September 1977, pages 260 and 323.

PAGE 145 Cuff and pair of heart earrings, autumn/winter 1992. Wood applied with gilt-metal flame motif; unsigned. Private collection
Note: Earrings like these appeared in an advertisement for Rive Gauche in October 1992. The model was wearing a brown beret, a tweed jacket, mid calf dark skirt and high-heeled Oxford shoes.

SCHIAPARELLI
"...dressmaker to whom...": "The Dressmakers of France," *Fortune*, 1932.
"house of ideas": *Harper's Bazaar*
"...order Schiaparelli's Cellophane...": Diana Vreeland, "Why Don't You," *Harper's Bazaar*, July 1936, page 78.
"...very much interested...": *Women's Wear Daily*, 1931.
"...an amusing little...": *Vogue*, January 1, 1940, page 73.

PAGE 146 Parasol, c. 1935. Petrol blue Bakelite, silk tulle and coq feathers; label: SCHIAPARELLI 21 PLACE VENDOME. Collection Mark Walsh

PAGE 147 Bear clip, Jean Schlumberger for Schiaparelli, Summer 1939. Gilt-metal with cream matte paint, faux ruby eyes, the nose ring set with rhinestones; signed: DÉPOSÉ. Collection Mark Walsh
Note: For an illustration of a bear clip, see: *Harper's Bazaar,* May 1939, page 139.

PAGE 148 Red straw visor, early to mid 1930s; label (red and white): 4 PLACE VENDOME PARIS. Collection Mark Walsh

PAGE 149 Fingernail gloves, autumn/winter 1936–1937. Black antelope with nails and fine piping of red snakeskin; unsigned. Philadelphia Museum of Art 69.232.55 Gift of Mme. Elsa Schiaparelli
Note: For an image of these gloves, see *Harper's Bazaar*, September 1936, page 67.

PAGE 149 Newsprint purse, summer 1935. Silk satin printed in black with a collage of reviews and notices in numerous languages, with fine piping and carrying handle of black satin. Among the elements is a Schiaparelli business card with her former address on the rue de la Paix crossed out and the new address 21, place Vendome Paris. Collection Mark Walsh
Note: Newsprint fabric made into folded newspaper beach hats were a feature of Schiaparelli's 1935 spring/summer collection, for an illustration, see *Harper's Bazaar*, May 1935, pages 86–87.

PAGE 150 Wedding veil, Circus collection, summer 1938. Ivory cotton tulle embroidered with bright blue bugle beads. Collection Philadelphia Museum of Art 1969.232.26, Gift of Mme. Elsa Schiaparelli
Note: "...with a circular veil...": Diana Vreeland, "Why Don't You," *Harper's Bazaar*, April 1938, page 103.

PAGE 150 Vanity case, c. 1935. Black antelope lined with shocking pink satin, with brass hardware; stamped in lower case: SCHIAPARELLI. Collection Museum of the City of New York 77.96, Donor: Mrs. James A. Thomas

PAGE 150 Attributed to Schiaparelli trompe l'oeil ermine tail scarf, 1938. Very long stole printed with ermine tail clusters and trimmed at the edges with ermine tails; unsigned. Collection Mark Walsh

PAGE 151 Jean Schlumberger for Schiaparelli ostrich hair pin, circus collection, summer 1938. Gilt-metal, painted pink, white and black, dangling glass beads of pale pink, darker pink and cornflower blue. Collection Mark Walsh/Leslie Chin

PAGE 151 Two harlequin clips, Commedia dell'Arte collection, mid season, spring 1939. Harlequin holding a bat, gilt-metal enameled in green, cream and violet/gray, marked: DÉPOSÉ. Harlequin with black mask, enameled in transparent red and opaque black, the collars and cuffs studded with rhinestones; marked: DÉPOSÉ. Collection Leslie Chin

PAGE 151 Musical trophy clip, music collection, autumn 1939. Enameled gilt metal, in the form of a trophy: guitar, viola, and drum tied with a pink and blue ribbon bow dangling a French horn, a lyre, bugle and harp; signed: DÉPOSÉ. Collection Mark Walsh
Note: For illustrations of musical trophy clips, see *Vogue*, June 1, 1939, page 53 and June 15, 1939, page 31 and *L'Officiel*, June 1939, page 37.

PAGE 151 Musical trophy gloves, music collection, autumn 1939. Purple silk embroidered with gilt-viola or cello tied with a yellow bow or with a silver and gold sequin edged tambourine, each embroidered around the wrist with a pink and white twisted ribbon tied in a trompe l'oeil bow; tiny label: SCHIAPARELLI PARIS. Collection Philadelphia Museum of Art 69.232.67ab Gift of Mme. Elsa Schiaparelli
Note: For a photograph of the matching purple silk evening dress embroidered around the hip line with a bugle, violin, French horn and harp, also belonging to the Philadelphia Museum of Art, Gift of Elsa Schiaparelli, see Palmer White, *Elsa Schiaparelli: Empress of Fashion*, New York: Rizzoli, 1986, 125.

PAGE 152 Victorian revival hat, c. 1938. Black watered silk trimmed with brown ostrich tipped in white and turquoise green velvet ribbons; label: SCHIAPARELLI 21, PLACE VENDOME, PARIS. Collection Mark Walsh

PAGE 152 Attributed to Schiaparelli pansy evening bag, c. 1937. Turquoise velvet three-dimensional petaled bag embroidered with round clear turquoise beads and short pearlescent turquoise tubes; the zipper of pale turquoise plastic and lighter green plastic with circle pull marked: LIGHTNING, unsigned. Collection Leslie Chin

PAGE 153 Attributed to Schiaparelli brocade evening bag, mid season collection 1937. Rayon brocade woven with a small floral pattern in shades of pale pink, blue, silver white and gray, trimmed with fine gilt leather piping, the clasp a gilt-metal hand holding a medium sized rose, sheer tint of pink for the petals and green for the leaves; unsigned. Collection Mark Walsh
Note: For an illustration of a foldover purse in purple calf fastening with a roseless hand, see *Harper's Bazaar*, December 1937, page 61, and *L'Officiel*, January 1938, page 82.

PAGE 153 Attributed to Schlumberger for Schiaparelli hand brooches, mid season collection 1937. Left: Gilt metal painted in black and translucent green; marked: DÉPOSÉ. Right: Gilt and silvertone metal, holding a rose bud and wearing a charm bracelet with tiny acorn, silvertone metal disc, pig; unsigned. Collection Leslie Chin
Note: "...buttons and clips...": *Women's Wear Daily*, October 28, 1937, section 1, page 2.

PAGE 153 Pansy clip, autumn/winter 1937. Gilt-metal set with faux pearls; signed: MADE IN FRANCE. Private collection
Note: Photographed for *Harper's Bazaar*, December 1937, page 92 "The much talked-of pansy clips to be worn with suits. One gold with purple, the other gold with orange."

PAGE 153 Attributed to Schiaparelli pansy parure, autumn/winter 1937. Bracelet, clip and double pansy pin of gilt-metal painted in shades of purple, periwinkle and lavender; one marked: PAT. 2066969. Provenance: Diana Vreeland. Courtesy Mark Walsh

PAGE 154 Mitts, summer 1938. Off-white satin with cut-out for thumb and dimpled metal buttons of different colors. Tiny label: SCHIAPARELLI PARIS. Collection Philadelphia Museum of Art 69.232.66, Gift of Mme. Elsa Schiaparelli
Note: Another pair of these mitts is in the collection of the Victoria & Albert Museum, donated by actress Ruth Ford, T412.1982.

PAGE 154 Hat, winter 1938–1939. Smoke blue felt with osprey feathers; label: SCHIAPARELLI HÎVER 1938–9 21, PLACE VENDOME PARIS. Collection Mark Walsh

PAGE 154 Taupe felt hat, autumn/winter 1937 with crinkled ribbon cockade, the underbrim edged with further ribbon; label: SCHIAPARELLI MADE IN FRANCE 21 PLACE VENDOME PARIS. Collection Mark Walsh

PAGE 154 Striped satin booties, winter 1939. Pink striped in green and silvery gray, mother-of-pearl buttons; stamped: PERUGIA POUR PADOVA 2, RUE DE LA PAIX PARIS. Philadelphia Museum of Art 69.232.57, Gift of Mme. Elsa Schiaparelli
Note: *Women's Wear Daily*, Thursday afternoon, October 27, 1938. For an image of boots like this, worn with an ankle length harem skirt of the same fabric, see *Vogue*, October 1, 1939, page 85.

PAGE 155 Attributed to Schiaparelli muff, c. spring/summer 1938. Red/purple silk interior and strap sewn with ombré silk violets, stems cut, unsigned. Provenance: Mrs. Arthur Conan Doyle, Cecil Beaton's sister. Collection Sandy Schreier

PAGE 156 Pine cone choker, spring/summer 1939. Gilt-metal hollow pine cones suspended from black velvet ribbon small bows sewn to cloth-of-gold ribbon; label: Made in France. Collection Mark Walsh/Leslie Chin.
Note: For a description of a necklace like this, see *Vogue*, March 15, 1939, page 52.

PAGE 156 Leaf necklace, 1937. Enameled gilt-metal, unsigned. Collection Karen Davidov
Note: For an image of a necklace like this, see: *Harper's Bazaar*, December 1937, page 92.

PAGE 156 Attributed to Schiaparelli evening gloves, c. spring/summer 1937. Deep cornflower blue silk chiffon trimmed with a single ocher velvet butterfly, its patterning stamped and printed in black, label in one: MADE IN FRANCE. Collection Mark Walsh
Note: "Butterflies flutter all through...": *Women's Wear Daily*, February 4, 1937, front page.

PAGE 157 Rose bib necklace, c. 1938. Silvertone metal painted in shades of dark red, pink and oyster; signed: MADE IN FRANCE. Collection Leslie Chin
Note: A similar necklace is in the collection of The Costume Institute, the Metropolitan Museum of Art, 1981.517.12, Gift of Beatrice Glass

PAGE 157 Attributed to Schiaparelli gardening tools necklace, c. 1939. Fuchsia velvet ribbon and enameled gilt-metal, the bucket spilling its contents of turquoise handled shears and sickle; unsigned. Collection Mark Walsh

PAGE 158 Beastly gloves, 1935. Astrakhan with palms of black suede; unsigned. Provenance: Annie Laurie Aitken. Collection Mark Walsh

PAGE 159 Schiaparelli monkey fur booties, winter 1939–1940. Black suede and monkey fur with black stacked heels; stamped: PERUGIA 2, RUE DE LA PAIX PARIS BREVETE S. B. D. G. Collection Philadelphia Museum of Art 69.232.55, Gift of Mme. Elsa Schiaparelli

PAGE 159 Schiaparelli leopard skin booties, winter 1939–1940. Collection Philadelphia Museum of Art 69.232.56, Gift of Mme. Elsa Schiaparelli
Note: Boots like these, described as bottines, were photographed for *Harper's Bazaar*, September 15, 1939, page 53.

VALENTINA
"jewelry should be real....flowers....shoes....a hat": *Harper's Bazaar*, January 1945, page 88.
"Simplicity survives the changes...": *The New York Times*, September 15, 1989.

PAGE 160 Coolie style hat, 1940s. Mustard plush felt lined with dark brown sheer silk; label: VALENTINA. Collection Museum of the City of New York 90.23.8, Donor: Estate of Valentina Schlee

PAGE 160 Tomato soup fine wool twill turban-fez, c. 1944–45; label: VALENTINA. Collection Museum of the City New York 86.63.4, Donor: Irene Worth

PAGE 161 Drawstring purse, 1940s. Dark green silk velvet, light green braid, and crocheted ball trim; label: VALENTINA. Provenance: Gloria Swanson. Private collection

PAGE 162 Black fur felt coolie hat. Embroidered with black cord scrolls and black faceted jet beads, the top knot of black braid and the underbrim sewn with further beads, black silk satin ribbon ties; label: VALENTINA. Provenance: Lillian Gish. Collection Sandy Schreier

VALENTINO
"The linings of...": Joan Juliet Buck, *Vogue*, March 1985, page 560.
"Inimmaginabile coordinato...": *Vogue Italia*, September 1983, page 461.

PAGE 162 Faux coral branch bib necklace, spring/summer 1991. Plastic coral branches, gilt-metal, faux mabe pearls and rhinestones;

unsigned. Private collection

PAGE 163   Sea star brooch, spring/summer 1996. Gilt and silvertone metal set with rhinestones and faux pearls; signed: V (in an oval). Collection Gwen Widell

PAGE 164   Greek vase brooch, c. 1990. White composition painted in black and cocoa and studded with small rhinestones. Collection Gwen Widell

PAGE 164   Pineapple brooch, spring/summer 1990. Gilt-metal set with two sizes of square rhinestones painted orange; unsigned. Collection Gwen Widell
Note: For a photograph of a pineapple brooch like this, worn with a paisley and check dress and waist-length check jacket, see Valentino advertisement, *British Vogue*, March 1990, page 29.

PAGE 165   Chain handled purse, c. 1991. Leopard printed haired calf, gilt-metal mount with stylized cats, gilt-metal chain handle; signed: VALENTINO GARAVANI MADE IN ITALY. Collection Kathy Irwin

GIANNI VERSACE

"Good taste...": *European Travel & Life*, June/July 1991, page 48.
"As always the...": *Women's Wear Daily*, Monday, February 28, 1983, section 1 page 9.

PAGE 166   Pop art print evening bag, spring/summer 1991. Printed ribbed cotton; handle of gilt-metal and glass beads in assorted colors; label: GIANNI VERSACE COUTURE. Collection Sandy Schreier

PAGE 167   Versace brooch, c. 1986. Silver tone metal, signed: GIANNI VERSACE MADE IN ITALY. Courtesy Doyle New York

PAGE 168   Ugo Correani for Gianni Versace "Machine Age" collar, c. 1988. Silver tone metal various shaped flowers set with rhinestones in shades of cornflower blue, light blue, amber, yellow, ruby and green, large clear rhinestones set in inner tube circles of colored glass; unsigned. Collection Sandy Schreier

PAGE 168   Ugo Correani for Gianni Versace asymmetric bib necklace, spring/summer 1999. Gilt-metal flowers set with multicolored rhinestones, gilt-metal links strung with pink, blue and green beads; metal tag: GIANNI VERSACE MADE IN ITALY. Collection Louise Doktor
Note: For a photograph of actress Kelly LeBrock wearing a similar necklace at a black tie tribute to Gianni

Versace held at the Century Plaza Hotel in Los Angeles, see *Harper's Bazaar*, May 1991, page 174.

PAGE 168   Safety pin backpack, 1994. Black napa leather with silvertone metal medusa head safety pins, label: GIANNI VERSACE COUTURE. Private collection

PAGE 169   Jewel handled pocketbook, spring/summer 1991. Pomegranate faux crocodile stamped leather with handle of gilt-metal and glass beads; label: GIANNI VERSACE COUTURE. Collection Kathy Irwin

MADELEINE VIONNET

"...developed a method...": Betty Kirke, MADELEINE VIONNET, San Francisco: Chronicle Books, 1998, pages 137–138.
"gold hair": *Vogue*, March 1, 1931, page 41.

PAGE 170   Evening headdress, mid-1930s. Silver lacquered straw curls, cream bird of paradise, black bird of paradise; unsigned. Original Vionnet box of glassine, marked: MADELEINE VIONNET 50, AVENUE MONTAIGNE (CHAMPS-ELYSEES), PARIS ACCESSOIRES. Collection Mark Walsh

PAGE 171   Boris Lacroix for Madeleine Vionnet. Cubist beaded envelope c. 1926–1929. Silver thread embroidery, gray and clear bugle beads, rhinestones. Collection The Metropolitan Museum of Art, the Costume Institute, Gift of Miriam Coletti 1985.364.13ab. Photograph by Karin L. Willis

PAGE 172   Boris Lacroix for Madeleine Vionnet handbag, c. 1928. Dark spinach green suede with carrying strap, single domed brass button clasp, interior of dark green satin, with two mirror pockets and coin purse. Labeled: MADELEINE VIONNET MODÈLE DÉPOSÉ. Collection Mark Walsh

PAGE 173   Brooch, c. 1933. Large faux emerald set in brass; marked: MADE IN FRANCE. The Metropolitan Museum, Costume Institute 1978.292 ab. Gift of Mr. and Mrs. Charles Abrams. Photograph by Karin L. Willis

PAGE 173   Madeleine Vionnet shoes with iron heels attributed to Jean Dunand, late 1920s. Caramel and brown leather stitched together in flat bands, fastening at the back of the heel with two yellow composition buttons; the heels of hammered iron made with a flower bud with top knot of leaves, the very

bottom of the shoe with a little leather disc to protect the floor and the shoe; stamped on the sole with circular insignia of a woman holding up her tunic and: MADELEINE VIONNET. Collection Mark Walsh

VIVIENNE WESTWOOD

"I would like...": *Vogue*, January 1995, page 128.

PAGE 174   Elevated satin slash shoes, "Dressing up" collection, autumn/winter 1991–1992. Black synthetic satin worked with Tudor slashes; stamped: MADE IN ENGLAND/VIVIENNE WESTWOOD/LONDON (with orb). Metropolitan Museum of Art, Costume Institute, 1997.59.3ab, Gift of the Estate of Luciana Martinez de la Rosa, 1997. Photograph by Karin L. Willis

PAGE 176   Denim hat, c. 2000; label: ANGLOMANIA VIVIENNE WESTWOOD SINCE 1990. Private collection

PAGE 176   Toe court shoe, "summertime collection" autumn/winter 2000–2001. French 18th-century-style floral brocade; printed in gilt: VIVIENNE WESTWOOD LONDON MADE IN ENGLAND. Private collection
Note: For runway images from the collection in which these shoes were shown, see *Collezioni*, Haute Couture Autumn/Winter 2000–2001, pages 165–174, various versions of the toe shoes, page 413, a jacket in the same brocade.

PAGE 177   Distressed gloves, autumn/winter 2000–2001. Moss green and lavender wool, embroidered multi colored and gilt orb symbol; label: VIVIENNE WESTWOOD. Private collection

SELECTED BIBLIOGRAPHY

BOOKS

Adburgham, Alison. *Liberty's: A Biography of a Shop*. London: George Allen & Unwin, Ltd., 1975.

Alaïa, Azzedine, Michel Tournier, et al. *Azzedine Alaïa*. Barbara Wright, trans. Göttingen: Steidl Publishers, 1998.

Baudot, François. *Alaïa*. London: Thames and Hudson, Ltd., 1996.

___. *Christian Lacroix*. Paris: Éditions Assouline, 1997.

___. *Elsa Schiaparelli*. Paris: Éditions Assouline, 1997.

Bergé, Pierre. *Yves Saint Laurent*. London: Thames and Hudson, Ltd., 1997.

Bertin Célia. *Paris à la Mode: A Voyage of Discovery*. Marjorie Deans, trans. Marial Deans, illus. London: Victor Gollancz, Ltd., 1956.

Bluttal, Steven, ed. *Halston*. London: Phaidon Press, Ltd., 2001.

Cera, Deanna Farneti, ed. *Jewels of Fantasy: Costume Jewelry of the 20th Century*. New York: Harry N. Abrams, Inc., 1991.

Charles-Roux, Edmonde. *Chanel and Her World*. London: Weidenfeld and Nicolson, 1981.

Chenoune, Farid. *Jean Paul Gaultier*. London: Thames and Hudson, 1996.

Coleman, Elizabeth Ann. *The Genius of Charles James*. New York: The Brooklyn Museum, 1982.

Cullerton, Brenda. *Geoffrey Beene*. New York: Harry N. Abrams, Inc., 1995.

de la Haye, Amy, and Shelley Tobin. *Chanel: The Couturiére at Work*. New York: The Overlook Press, 1994.

Delasandres, Yvonne. *Poiret: Paul Poiret 1879–1944*. Paula Clifford, trans. New York: Rizzoli, 1987.

Demornex, Jacqueline. *Madeline Vionnet*. Augusta Audubert, trans. New York: Rizzoli, 1991.

Duras, Marguerite, et al. *Yves Saint Laurent: Images of Design 1958–1988*. New York: Alfred A. Knopf, Inc., 1988.

Giroud, Françoise, and Sacha Van Dorssen. *Dior*. New York: Rizzoli, 1987.

Guillaume, Valérie. *Jacques Fath*. Paris: Éditions Paris-Museés/Société nouvelle Adam Biro, 1993.

Holborn, Mark. *Issey Miyake*. Köln: Benedikt Taschen Verlag GmbH, 1995.

Jouve, Marie-Andrée, and Jacqueline Demornex. *Balenciaga*. New York: Rizzoli, 1989.

Keenan, Brigid. *Dior in Vogue*. New York: Harmony Books, 1981.

Kirke, Betty. *Madeline Vionnet*. San Francisco: Chronicle Books, 1998.

Koda, Harold. *Extreme Beauty: The Body Transformed*. New York: The Metropolitan Museum of Art and Yale University Press, 2001.

Koda, Harold, Germano Celant, Susan Cross, and Karole Vail. *Armani*. New York: Guggenheim Museum Publications, 2000.

Krell, Gene. *Vivienne Westwood*. Paris: Éditions Assouline, 1997.

Leymarie, Jean. *Chanel*. Jean-Marie Clark, trans. New York: Rizzoli, 1987.

Martin, Richard. *Fashion and Surrealism*. New York: Fashion Institute of Technology, 1987.

Mauriès, Patrick. *Christian Lacroix: The Diary of a Collection*. Jane Brenton, trans. New York: Simon & Schuster Editions, 1996.

___. *Jewelry by Chanel*. London: Thames and Hudson, Ltd., 1993.

McDowell, Colin. *Jean Paul Gaultier*. New York: Viking Studio, 2001.

___. *Manolo Blahnik*. New York: HarperCollins, 2000.

Milbank, Caroline Rennolds. *Couture: The Great Designers*. New York: Stewart, Tabori, and Chang, 1985.

___. *New York Fashion: The Evolution of American Style*. New York: Harry N. Abrams, Inc., 1989.

Miyake, Issey. *Issey Miyake: East Meets West*. Tokyo: Heibonsha Limited, 1978.

Morris, Bernadine. *Valentino*. Paris: Éditions Assouline, 1996.

Moschino, Franco, and Lida Castelli. *X Anni di Kaos!*. Milan: Edizioni Lybra Immagine, 1993.

Piaggi, Anna. *Anna Piaggi's Fashion Algebra*. Cecilia Treves, trans. London: Thames and Hudson, Ltd., 1998.

___. *Lagerfeld's Sketchbook: Karl Lagerfeld's Illustrated Fashion Journal of Anna Piaggi*. London: Thames and Hudson, Ltd., New York: Weidenfeld and Nicolson, 1986.

Pringle, Colombe. *Roger Vivier*. Paris: Éditions Assouline, 1998.

Richards, Melissa. *Chanel: Key Collections*. London: Welcome Rain Publishers, 2000.

Saint Laurent, Yves, Pierre Bergé, and Hélène de Turckheim. *Yves Saint Laurent par Yves Saint Laurent*. Paris: Éditions Herscher, 1986.

Trasko, Mary. *Heavenly Soles: Extraordinary Twentieth-Century Shoes*. New York: Abbeville Press, 1989.

Tsurumoto, Shōzō, ed. *Issey Miyake Bodyworks*. Tokyo: Shogakukan Publishing Co., Ltd., 1983.

Vecchio, Walter. *The Fashion Makers: A Photographic Record*. Robert Riley, text. New York: Crown Publishers, Inc., 1968.

Vermorel, Fred. *Vivienne Westwood: Fashion, Perversity, and the Sixties Laid Bare*. New York: The Overlook Press, 1996.

Wallach, Janet. *Chanel: Her Style and Her Life*. New York: Nan A. Talese, Doubleday, 1998.

White, Palmer. *Poiret*. New York: Clarkson N. Potter, Inc., 1973.

___. *Elsa Schiaparelli: Empress of Fashion*. New York: Rizzoli, 1986.

Yohannan, Kohle, and Nancy Nolf. *Claire McCardell: Redefining Modernism*. New York: Harry N. Abrams, Inc., 1998.

___. *Bijoux de Haute Couture: Collection Robert Goossens*. Paris: Éditions Plume, 2000.

EXHIBITION CATALOGUES

"Hommage à Balenciaga." Museé Historique des Tissus de Lyon. September 28, 1985–January 6, 1986. Paris: Éditions Herscher, 1985.

"Christian Dior." The Costume Institute at the Metropolitan Museum of Art. New York, December 12, 1996–March 23, 1997. New York: The Metropolitan Museum of Art, 1996.

"Hommage à Christian Dior, 1947–1957." Museé des Arts de la Mode. Paris, March 19–October 4, 1987. Paris: Union des Arts Décoratifs, 1986.

"Givenchy: 40 Ans de Création." Le Palais Galliera. Paris, 1991. Paris: Paris-Museés, 1991.

"Givenchy: 30 Years." Fashion Institute of Technology. New York, May 10–October 2, 1982.

"Issey Miyake: Pleats Please." Touko Museum of Contemporary Art. September 1–30, 1990. Tokyo: Touko Museum of Contemporary Art, 1990.

"Jacqueline Kennedy: The White House Years" The Costume Institute at the Metropolitan Museum of Art. May 1–July 29, 2001. New York: The Metropolitan Museum of Art.

"Elsa Peretti: Fifteen of My Fifty." Fashion Institute of Technology. New York, April 24–May 10, 1990.

"Yves Saint Laurent." The Costume Institute at the Metropolitan Museum of Art. New York, December 14, 1983–September 2, 1984. New York: The Metropolitan Museum of Art, 1983.

"Hommage à Elsa Schiaparelli." Museé de la Mode et du Costume, Palais Galléria. Paris, June 21–August 30, 1984.

"Gianni Versace." The Costume Institute at the Metropolitan Museum of Art. New York, December 11, 1997–March 22, 1998. New York: The Metropolitan Museum of Art, 1997.

AUCTION CATALOGUES

"Sale of the Personal Collection of Chanel." Christie's, London, December 2, 1978.

"Couture Jewels: The Designs of Robert Goossens." Christie's East, New York, November 15, 2000.

"The Estate of Jacqueline Kennedy Onassis." Sotheby's, New York, April 23–26, 1996.

"The Diana Vreeland Collection of Fashion Jewelry." Sotheby's, New York, October 21, 1987.

PERIODICALS

L'Art et la mode
Avenue
Collections Gap
Collezioni
Departures
Elle (American and French editions)
Esquire
European Travel & Life
Femina
Flair
Harper's Bazaar
Harpers and Queen
International Herald Tribune
Interview
Mirabella
La Mode en Peinture
Life
The Metropolitan Museum of Art Bulletin
The New York Times
The New York Times Magazine
New York Woman
The New Yorker
Newsweek
L'Officiel
L'Officiel 1000 Modèles
Le Supplement aux Collections de la haute couture de Paris
Taxi
Time
Town & Country
Vanity Fair
Vogue (American, British, French, and Italian editions)
W
Women's Wear Daily
WWD/Global

Acknowledgments

Project Manager: Eric Himmel
Senior Editor: Harriet Whelchel
Designer: Tsang Seymour Design
Photo Stylist: Lai Ngan Corio
Production Manager: Alyn Evans

Library of Congress Cataloging-in-Publication Data

Milbank, Caroline Rennolds.
The couture accessory / by Caroline Rennolds Milbank.
p. cm.
Includes index.
ISBN 0-8109-3534-1
1. Dress accessories. 2. Costume design—History. 3. Fashion
designers—History. I. Title.
TT560 .M55 2002
746.9'2—dc21
2002002449

Text copyright © 2002 Caroline Rennolds Milbank
Photographs copyright © 2002 David Corio, unless otherwise
credited in the List of Illustrations

Published in 2002 by Harry N. Abrams, Incorporated, New York
All rights reserved. No part of the contents of this book may be
reproduced without the written permission of the publisher.

Printed and bound in Italy
10 9 8 7 6 5 4 3 2 1

Harry N. Abrams, Inc.
100 Fifth Avenue
New York, N.Y. 10011
www.abramsbooks.com

Abrams is a subsidiary of

LA MARTINIÈRE
G R O U P E

To all those who joined in making this a thoroughly enjoyable project, I am deeply indebted. At Harry N. Abrams, Inc, I am grateful to Margaret Chace, Eric Himmel, Michael Walsh, and, most especially, my editor, Harriet Whelchel. For their gorgeous teamwork, not to mention photographs, thanks to: David Corio, photographer, and Lai Ngan Corio, stylist. Many thanks for additional photographs to: Karin L. Willis, the Photography Studio, The Metropolitan Museum of Art, and Jérôme Schlomoff in Paris. For the elegance of their creation, I thank Catarina Tsang and Laura Howell at Tsang Seymour.

Research, always a delicious process, was greatly aided by Jennifer Cole and by Stéphane Houy-Towner. Thanks also to Dilys Blum, Steven Bluttal, Deirdre Donohue, Marie Andrée Jouve, Betty Kirke, Laura Layfer, Tatyana Pakhladzhyan, and Natalia Rand.

Crucial beyond measure have been the owners of all the fascinating objects we borrowed to study and photograph. Endless gratitude to Sandy Schreier, whose couture collection has always had a strong focus on accessories and who answered just about every question of what I was looking for with "I've got it." Mark Walsh and Leslie Chin not only provided marvelous pieces but continually offered clues as to objects' whereabouts. For their suggestions, leads, connections, generosity, and, especially, exquisite taste I thank: Teri Agins, Iris Apfel, Mary Baskett, Deeda Blair, Bunny Bodman, Holly Brubach, Amy Fine Collins, Kendra and Allan Daniel, Karen Davidov, Tian Dayton, Louise Doktor, Noella Facchinetti, Christy Ferer, Ella Milbank Foshay, Isabel Fowlkes, Cara Friemann, Titi Halle, Kathleen Hearst, Linda Hickox, Miki Higasa, Cathy Horyn, Kathy Irwin, Adeline Tintner Janowitz, Jun Kanai, Christie Mayer Lefkowith, Jane Trapnell Marino, Molly Milbank, Lars Nillson, Patricia Pastor, Joan Phillips, Joan Raines, Amelie Rives Rennolds, Zandra Rhodes, Margery Rubin, Clementine Sainty, Beatrice Santo Domingo, Marina Schiano, and Gwen Widell.

Some of the most spectacular items in the book come from fashion designers' archives. For the loan of these treasures, I thank: Azzedine Alaïa: Fabien Mage; Giorgio Armani: Jenna Barnet, Paula Decato, Linda Gaunt; Geoffrey Beene: Russell Nardozza; Jean Paul Gaultier: Hélèna Sipicki, Patricia Muller; Christian Lacroix: Marie Martinez; Moschino: Amy Marth; Issey Miyake: Nancy S. Knox; Yves Saint Laurent: Dominique Deroche, and Connie Uzzo.

Not only did the following institutions graciously lend objects to be photographed but their collections were invaluable in terms of research. I am grateful to: The Bruce Museum, Greenwich: Nancy Hall-Duncan; The Museum at F. I. T.: Valerie Steele and Fred Dennis; The Metropolitan Museum of Art Costume Institute: Harold Koda, Lisa Faibish, Karin L. Willis, Emily Martin, Alexandra Kowalski, Melinda Webber; The Philadelphia Museum of Art: Dilys Blum; Wadsworth Atheneum: Carol Krute. At Doyle New York, many thanks to: Linda Donahue, Kathy Doyle, Jan Reeder, and Louis LeB. Webre

Not a day goes by that I don't miss my parents in a myriad of ways. Among their many treasured qualities were that they were walking reference libraries. In their absence the following people have contributed information, support, amusing facts, simultaneous translation, seemingly unflagging interest in the progress of the book, and/or writing companionship. Many thanks to: Teri Agins, Geoffrey Beene, Dilys Blum, Margaret Chace, Mary Crenshaw, Karen d´Amore, Anne Freeman, Anne Goldrach, Titi Halle, Margot Horsey, Phyllis Magidson, Buffy Morgan, and, especially, Harold Koda. Absolutely pivotal has been the group consisting of: Barbara Canner, Blair Fowlkes Childs, Paulette Cushman, Isabel Fowlkes, Nettie Fowlkes, Diane Lyon, Bannon McHenry, Virginia Thors, and Arete Warren. For her Christmas miracle, thanks to Gina Bianco; for technical help: Jo Duer; for time to think: Luzvimin Amancio, for everything, always: Jerry Milbank.